DELIVER ME FROM *Adam*

EDDI

Unless otherwise noted, Scripture quotations are from *THE NEW KING
JAMES VERSION.* Copyright 1979, 1980, 1982, Thomas Nelson, Inc.,
Publishers.

ISBN 1586029002

Produced by Truth Communications, www.realtruth.tv
Printed in the United States of America.

I dedicate this book to my Lord and Savior, Jesus Christ.

I also dedicate this to my wife, Vanessa, my sons Eric, Edward and Jared, and my daughter Taylor—thank you for unselfishly allowing me to give myself to the world. I want to also give a special thanks to the New Birth Missionary Baptist Church congregation in Lithonia, Georgia.

DELIVER ME FROM ADAM

Contents

Acknowledgments

I had just finished preaching the final service of the Harvest Conference in Charleston, WV and sat slumped in a chair in Bishop Jakes' office. We were discussing various Kingdom issues when, out of nowhere he said, "There is someone you need to meet". He picked up the phone, dialed a number and handed me the receiver. That was a long time ago…but I still remember the overwhelming sense of love that swept over me when Bishop Eddie Long responded to my "Hello I'm Mark Hanby" by replying; "I'm blessed to meet you Mark, when can you come to Atlanta…I need you".

Through the years I have come to understand that this unpretentious humble man of God did not really "need" me so much, but was simply expressing his normal open hearted desire to seek pure relationship without the need to impress or control. In truth Bishop Eddie Long's investment in our relationship, through good times and bad has abundantly exceeded anything that I have been able to offer. He simply knows who he is and doesn't keep score.

I was therefore not surprised when I first perused the manuscript Deliver Me From Adam. This is not just another self-help script. This is the essence of a man's life, the expression of his heart. This book Deliver Me From Adam is the product of process, the picture of applied and practiced principles. The pages of this epistle are ablaze with the torch of truth, lit by the pin of a scribe who has escaped the tyranny of the old Adam, having discovered the liberty so abundant in Christ.

Finally, someone has thoroughly addressed the issue of our greatest struggle; the loss of our true identity and the crying need for redemptive recovery. We are reminded again that in spite of our human frailty, we are God's greatest treasure.

As you read these pages with an open heart and mind you will become aware, as I have, that Bishop Long is giving us keys, Kingdom keys, that unlock the prison of the mind, truly delivering us from Adam.

- Pastor Mark Hanby

Foreword

If you have ever wondered how to get from where you are and what you are doing to what God has purposed for you to be and become, Deliver Me From Adam is the book for you. You will discover how to go from victim to victor, from self-centered to selfless, and from being overcome to becoming an overcomer.

If repentance is not in your vocabulary, it will be. If your own actions, thoughts, and motives are not on the altar, get ready to put them there in an honest appraisal before God, because transformation is just ahead.

Like a caterpillar metamorphisizing into a butterfly, the process of change won't be easy, and it won't be pretty, but it is necessary for the revolution that must take place, beginning in each of us.

This is not just another compilation of catchy phrases from Dr. Feelgood, nor a cleverly packaged message from some theological theorist who has never placed a hand of healing and hope on the heart of stricken humanity. Bishop Eddie Long is a man who proclaims the heartbeat of God not only with his words, but with his life.

As you read, I believe your expectation will be the same as mine – Lord, Deliver Me From Adam!

- Pastor Rod Parsley

Introduction

Some people call wisdom by another name—*hindsight*. We have one homespun proverb that says, "Hindsight is 20/20" (meaning we see things with perfect vision after we've already messed things up and gone another 20 years or so down the road of life).

The Apostle Paul told the Corinthian Christians, "When I was a child, I spoke as a child, I understood as a child, I thought as a child; but when I became a man, I put away childish things. For now we see in a mirror, dimly, but then face to face. Now I know in part, but then I shall know just as I also am known" (1 Cor. 13:11-12, emphasis mine).

I've been looking into my mirror for more than a half century now. Some of the steam of my youth has cleared away, but the need for reading glasses has complicated my view instead. The titles attached to the man in the mirror have changed over time...man, husband, father, pastor, and now bishop—but my march through time continues to improve my spiritual vision.

With the invaluable help of the Holy Spirit, my understanding of image has suddenly taken on a new shape and importance. More pieces of the life puzzle came together and vital truths from God's unchanging Word came alive as never before.

I see more clearly now—*we must be delivered from Adam to live in Christ*. What used to be a tangled mess has now come into focus. This battle of images and identities, and our misunderstanding of it literally entangles our lives and hinders our progress as followers of Christ and builders of the Kingdom of God.

4   As a leader in Christ's church and God's Kingdom, part of my assignment is to help others put together the "jigsaw puzzle" of life using the illumination of God's Word and the Holy Spirit.

In humility and with thankfulness to our Lord, I offer this freshly finished "corner of the puzzle" to you. If you have longed to break free from the fog of confusion over "wanting to do good but actually doing bad" in life, then you may find help in these pages.

Our hope does not rest in Adam's image passed down from the shadow of the tree in the Garden of Eden—it is found in the image of Christ given to each of us in the shadow of the tree on Mount Calvary.

May the truth of God fully deliver you from Adam and enfold you in the image of Christ. This isn't theology packaged in a book; it is freedom in a *Name* that is higher than every name.

Bishop Eddie L. Long
Atlanta, Georgia
April, 2004

And being found in appearance as a man, He humbled Himself and became obedient to the point of death, even the death of the cross. Therefore God also has highly exalted Him and given Him the name which is above every name, that at the name of Jesus every knee should bow, of those in heaven, and of those on earth, and of those under the earth, and that every tongue should confess that Jesus Christ is Lord, to the glory of God the Father. Therefore, my beloved, as you have always obeyed, not as in my presence only, but now much more in my absence, work out your own salvation with fear and trembling; for it is God who works in you both to will and to do for His good pleasure (Phil. 2:5-13).

Chapter 1

Lord, Deliver Me From Adam!

Something happened to me when I turned 50.

Looking back from the half-century mark, it was painful to admit that I still hadn't reached the "best" God had for me yet. Jesus defined true living when He said, "I have come that they *may have life,* and that they may have it *more abundantly*" (John 10:10b, emphasis mine). The truth is that very few of us really live this way.

My job titles may read bishop and pastor, but after some strong soul-searching and honest wrestling with the Lord, I knew something had to change. I want more of the abundant life God promises. I refuse to go out of this life "living dead."

You may not be anywhere near my age milestone, but how would you describe your life right now? Is it an abundant life, a journey of struggle, or a song of sorrows?

Perhaps you picked up this book because you do not believe your life (or the life of the Church) is everything it should be. Honestly, are you really experiencing what God's Word calls the "more abundant" life?

Every time I search the Scriptures, I see God calling us to be living testimonies in a messed up world. The church seems to be better at displaying a messed up testimony to a distrusting world.

I've had some success as a disciple of God and a Christian leader, but I am not content to remain where I am. When I see the fullness of God's promise for the "more abundant life," then I know I want more than I have or live right now.

You may be thinking, "Well, aren't you a 'bishop'? If you can't measure up, if you can't say you have arrived, then who can?" Remember that bishops, pastors, and presidents all put their pants on one leg at a time. Some of us may be further along in the process of godliness, but we all tend to fall into the same ditches from time to time.

Paul the apostle described the biggest of these ditches:

> "For I delight in the law of God according to the inward man. But I see another law in my members, warring against the law of my mind, and bringing me into captivity to the law of sin which is in my members. *O wretched man that I am! Who will deliver me from this body of death?"* (Rom. 7:22-24, emphasis mine).

Can You Conceive of a Life Without Condemnation?

This couldn't be the great apostle of the faith speaking to us! Didn't he write 13 epistles in the New Testament? Why is he calling himself a wretched man? If he couldn't make it, how can I?

Let Paul answer for himself. Read on:

> "I thank God; through Jesus Christ our Lord! So then, with the mind I myself serve the law of God, but with the flesh the law of sin. There is therefore now *no condemnation* to those who are in Christ Jesus, who do not walk according to the flesh [the old Adam nature], but according to the Spirit [of the Second Adam]. For the law of the *Spirit of life in Christ Jesus* has made me free from the law of sin and death" (Rom. 7:25–8:2, emphasis mine).

Can you conceive of a life without condemnation? God offers everyone the same toolbox and instructions for fixing and maintaining their lives. It contains the miracle of Jesus Christ and the cross along with the truths of God's Word.

God also gives everyone in His Kingdom the same job **9** description: Be fishers of men, be lovers of God and one another, and be holy. You show up with your body, soul, and spirit, and I will provide everything else.

The problem is that we show up at church and leave week after week; but we look, act, and live just like people who have never been to church or received Jesus Christ as Savior.

The Abundant Life is More Than Outward Things

What will it take for people to genuinely see Jesus in us? On my 50th birthday, I acknowledged a sobering fact: it would take more than what I have right now.

People should notice that we are different—even without the help of gold lapel pins, Bibles the size of library dictionaries, or loud shouts of "Hallelujah" in the mall. I have nothing against any of these things, but surely the abundant life God promises is more than the outward things we wear, carry, or say!

I heard someone define mental illness as "the habit of always doing the same things while expecting different results." Isn't that what most of us do day after day and year after year?

I'm ready for a change, but that means I have to be willing to change myself.

Twenty-five words from Jesus in the Gospel of John have literally rocked my life and ignited an explosion of change in my life. My obsession with these words led me to write this book:

"You did not choose Me, but I chose you and appointed you that you should *go and bear fruit*, and that your *fruit should remain...* " (John 15:16a, emphasis mine).

Jesus Christ wants more than a part-time production of "fruit" on the tree of your life. It is good to have "fruit" in your life, but it takes more to match God's definition of true success, and fruit alone doesn't prove you are walking in your destiny.

> **Every time you experience unending cycles of failure and defeat in your life, you will find "Adam" behind it somewhere!**

According to Jesus, He is looking for an abundance of fruit that remains—that means He expects to see something that will stick around even after you're gone.

That's the mark we shoot for; that is what it means to live the abundant life. It means that your children are taken care of. It means you made provisions for your children's children. It even means your neighborhood is cared for (even after you die).

I don't claim to be perfect, but this fresh revelation of the role "Adam" played in my daily struggles has revolutionized my life and ministry. It began with this amazing discovery: *Every time you experience unending cycles of failure and defeat in your life, you will find "Adam" behind it somewhere!*

God has an answer for what ails us. He is calling each of us to grow in maturity and effectiveness as disciples. (That means that at times He will touch some things you really don't want Him to disturb!)

What I am about to say may "mess" with your spirituality and preset ideas about religion: throughout the history of time and the human race, there have been only two men. In other words, there are only two "Adams" or points of human origin in the Bible.

The first Adam was the first created man and human "son" of God to exist on the earth. Jesus Christ is the Second Adam, and the one and only begotten Son of God.

We are either *of Adam* or we are *of Christ*. I don't think most people know that there's such a gap between Adam and

Christe, and even fewer people realize how "stuck" we are in   **11**
the old Adam.

You could be a charter member of your local church
or even a deacon, elder, or bishop in your religious circles—
but you are either of Adam or of Christ.

Describe it any way you like—"the proof is in the
pudding." "What you see is what you get." "It's what you do
more than what you say"—but the principle is still true.
The Apostle Paul said, "For as in Adam all die, even so in
Christ all shall be made alive" (1 Cor. 15:22).

Did you realize you can get "saved" for eternity and
still *live dead*? God is looking for fruit in your life. Is your life
producing "dead fruit" or "saved fruit"?

How do you know? Ask yourself, "How do the people who
work with me view my life? Who do I resemble the most?
Fallen Adam or the Risen Adam?"

Even though you show up every time the church doors
open, you can still walk dead, talk dead, and act dead. If we
examine the fruit, it appears
that most of the people who
"go to church" in the western
world are dead.

I'm not trying to pass
judgment on their eternal
destination; I am focusing the
light of God's Word on their
outward or visible lives. You
and I are the only "Bible" many
people will ever read. What

> **If we examine
> the fruit, it
> appears that
> most of the people
> who "go to church"
> in the western
> world are dead.**

they see in our lives may be the only introduction to God they
will ever have.

From the viewpoint of people outside of the church world,
"born-again" Christians get divorced just as often or *more*
often than unsaved people! We seem to lie, cheat, steal,
commit adultery, break our commitments, and abandon our
families just as often as "sinners." We may not kill people
physically, but we stab our brothers and sisters in the back over

12 and over again each day with our words and attitudes.

Paul describes our situation in the book of 1 Corinthians:

> "There is a natural body, and there is a spiritual body. And so it is written, "The first man Adam became a living being." The last Adam became a life-giving spirit. However, the spiritual is not first, but the natural, and afterward the spiritual. The first man was of the earth, made of dust; the second Man is the Lord from heaven" (1 Cor. 15:44b-47, emphasis mine).

Deliver Me From Adam! This Image Is Killing Me!

These verses should launch a life-changing revolution in the way we live as Christians. They helped transform the lives of thousands of Christians who attend New Birth Missionary Baptist Church where I serve as senior pastor.

As I approached my 50th birthday, I reread Paul's words to the Corinthians and I began to cry out to the Lord, *"Deliver me from Adam! This image is killing me!"*

Whether you are 50, 75, 15, or 25, I urge you to release God's transformation process in your own life right now by praying this prayer:

> *"Lord, deliver me from Adam. I don't want to die; I want to live. I am not going to die, but I shall live. Deliver me from Adam, in Jesus' name. Amen.*

As a man, a husband, and a father, I want to fulfill everything God said about me. As a Christian, as a member of a local church, and as a church leader, I am determined to see us fulfill—as a corporate body—everything God has said about us from the beginning.

The only way we can fulfill God's dream for us is to be delivered from Adam's nightmare. All we received from

Adam's bloodline was a heritage of bondage. Paul described it   **13**
this way:

> "For those who live according to the flesh set their
> minds on the things of the flesh, but those who live
> according to the Spirit, the things of the Spirit. For to
> be carnally minded [living out Adam's nightmare] is
> death, but to be spiritually minded [living out God's
> dream] is life and peace" (Rom. 8:5-6).

Are You Living Adam's Nightmare or God's Dream?

Freedom comes only when we make decisions to receive
and live in what Jesus, the Second Adam has done for us.

My concern is that many "saved and sanctified saints"
continue to relive Adam's nightmare rather than enjoy God's
dream. There is so much darkness and dissent in the church
today that many of us miss the life God intends for us. Refresh
your picture of God's vision for your life:

> "I have come that they *may have life,* and that they
> may have it *more abundantly"* (John 10:10b, emphasis
> mine).

Too many of us are missing the *life* God intended.
Remember Paul's insight in God's Word: "For as in Adam all
die, even so in Christ all shall be made alive" (1 Cor. 15:22).

Most people live at the mercy of their circumstances —
and that includes church people, unsaved people, black
people, white people, brown people, and rich and poor people
too. Their lives are constantly messed up or propped up by
"outside" situations, circumstances, people, and events. I call
these outside things "Adam stuff."

If you ask people "who they are," the answer seems
to change with the weather or with the ever-changing
circumstances of their lives. When there's money in their

14 pocket, booze in their glass, dope in their bag, or a date on their arm, they may feel on top of the world. The moment these things are gone, so is their happiness.

Never Define Who You are by What You See and Experience

This problem isn't new...it contaminated and doomed Adam and Eve at the beginning in the Garden of Eden.

> **"So when the woman saw that the tree was good for food, that it was pleasant to the eyes, and a tree desirable to make one wise, she took of its fruit and ate. She also gave to her husband with her, and he ate. Then the eyes of both of them were opened, and they knew that they were naked; and they sewed fig leaves together and made themselves coverings"** (Gen. 3:6-7).

We may be tempted to say Eve was "like us," but the truth is that we are "like Eve." She was influenced to define what she was or what she wasn't by what she saw and experienced.

She saw that the forbidden tree was (1) good for food, (2) pleasant to the eyes, and (3) desirable to make one wise. The combined attraction of all of these benefits was strong, but one promised "benefit" seemed to outweigh everything else.

The Garden of Eden was beautiful from one end to the other. It was packed with good food to eat, and the place was filled with beautiful things that were pleasant to look at. That meant that the first two temptations should have had no affect on Eve.

What really hooked Eve was the forbidden "knowledge of good and evil" (see Gen. 2:17 for God's exact warning to Adam). The serpent added to God's words to produce just the right bait to entrap an entire race in sin. He told Eve, "...in the day you eat of it your eyes will be opened, and you will be like God, knowing good and evil" (Gen. 3:5).

God didn't say that—the serpent did. First the deceiver told Eve what she was not, and then he implied that she needed the very thing God said would be fatal to her. He still uses the same lie today.

Eve fell for the con job and desired to be what the serpent told her she was not. She wanted to "be like God" and "know good and evil." (She didn't realize that she and Adam together had already been created in the very image and likeness of God!)

Most of us Live to Impress

I'm convinced the only reason most people say they want to "be wise" is so that they can impress somebody else. Most of us live to impress, and if we can't impress somebody then we aren't alive.

That helps explain why Christians are so mean to one another in church. Perhaps we are too busy being hypocrites trying to impress other people to even know who we really are.

Human history took its first step toward death when Eve discarded God's Word and reached for the forbidden fruit (it was really death on a stick). It took the second fatal step when Eve gave the forbidden fruit to her husband.

Adam bears the greater blame because he knew what was right, but he didn't *do* what was right. Why did he do it? He was afraid of what Eve might say or think. Most of us still do what Adam did.

We know what is right but we are afraid to do it. Why? We choose to give in to peer pressure and conform to the opinions and expectations of other people rather than to the gentle call of God to conform to the image of Christ in our hearts.

Are you more worried about what people think than about what God has said? Are you obsessed with the details of what people think about the clothes you wear to church, the kind of car you drive, the social status of your close friends, or how you worship God in public?

The Old Adam Drives us to Seek Approval

The truth is that it doesn't matter what people think about your worship! Worship is for God, not for us. As for the rest of that stuff, who will care in a month what you wore or drove to church this week?

In the old Adam state, we are driven to constantly seek approval from others. In fact, most of our inner hurts can be traced to our feelings of rejection because someone didn't like us or openly disapproved of something we did. Step back and get a new view of this situation.

David expressed the attitude God approves when he said:

"I will praise You, for I am fearfully and wonderfully made; marvelous are Your works, and that my soul knows very well. My frame was not hidden from You, when I was made in secret, and skillfully wrought in the lowest parts of the earth" (Ps. 139:14-15).

If you and I were fearfully, wonderfully, and skillfully made by God; then why do we allow jealous and ignorant remarks said about us by some little earthbound joker to just mess up our lives?

Who Outranks God in Your Life?

The words, actions, and opinions of others will only affect us if we value those things more than the words, actions, and opinions of God. If we put God first in all things, then what He says, does, and thinks about us should outweigh everything and everyone else. If they don't, then somebody is outranking God in our lives. It is that simple. Who outranks God in your life?

One of the favorite complaints we hear from new Christians is, "Friends don't treat me the way they used to." Well, they shouldn't. If we truly repent of an ungodly lifestyle, then why should we expect old friends to offer us drinks and drugs the way they used to? They shouldn't be asking you to "come hang out with Sally" when you are married to Sue.

The problem is that we want to keep one foot in God's Kingdom and one foot in Adam's world. The Bible calls it being "double minded." We want all of the benefits of being saved but we also want to be treated like we aren't. The Bible says, "A double minded man is unstable in all his ways" (Jas. 1:8, KJV).

We pattern all of our thinking and behavior in anticipation of a response from people around us.

"What will she say if I do this, I wonder?"

"Will my friends still accept me if I stop doing what they are doing?"

We feel hurt if we don't get the response we anticipated in our minds. I wish I could say that this problem doesn't exist in the church, but I can't. There are more "hurt" and offended folk inside the church than there are outside. We seem to get offended over the smallest things. "I saved her a seat and she didn't even say thank you."

As Christians, we should examine our motives continually. "Am I doing what I'm doing because I want to win friends and influence people to think a certain way about me? Was I networking when God wanted me tending His nets? Was I just trying to get a phone number?"

Adam Operates From a Fear Basis

As long as we stay in the Adam state, nearly everything is done from a fear basis. When you finally get to the root of it, most people are scared! It shows up in the form of worry. We worry when things don't go the way we want them to go we worry when we feel out of control and at the mercy of things, circumstances, and people we cannot control.

Some of us battle what we feel is an intense need for external power. We just have to be recognized. "I've got to have power."

18 Jesus sees things differently. In His Kingdom, love is the primary characteristic we should display. He said:

> **"A new commandment I give to you, that you love one another; as I have loved you, that you also love one another. By this all will know that you are My disciples, if you have love for one another"** (John 13:34-35).

Why is it so difficult for unsaved people to pick out church people who, supposedly, are His disciples? Perhaps it is because what we call "love" is often manipulation masquerading as something it is not.

Is It Love or Manipulation Behind a Mask?

Too many of us manipulate people in the name of love. We try to control people—either openly or without realizing it. Many times, we gather a circle of people around us who tend to yield to our control and do things "our way."

You may not agree that most people play the manipulation game, but we all expect certain responses from the people around us.

Throughout our lives, we tend to do the "Adam thing" by determining our actions and responses according to what does or does not happen externally. Some of that is normal—if a payment is due, you respond by paying. If it rains, you make adjustments.

The problem comes when we base our joy and happiness on our circumstances and approval of others. If things go wrong, we lose our joy. The "Adam" in us wants to maintain this artificial joy by manipulating the environment. We get sad if we can't manipulate our circumstances, spouses, bosses, or friends.

(By the way, a real friend cannot be manipulated. A friend stays with you in good times and bad, whether you are having a good day or just want to roll over and sleep until a better day comes along.)

Firmly planted beneath our desire for approval and control, there is a bedrock of fear. We fear rejection, failure, loneliness, and pain. Most of us are secretly afraid that if people ever manage to figure us out and discover the "real" us behind the masks, then they will reject or dominate us.

We often see it exposed in "macho" men who try to act tough in public situations. Any man who tries to act tough—especially a man who physically abuses his spouse or children—is absolutely afraid of life. He is so afraid of exposure that he resorts to manipulating and controlling his environment through brute force.

Want Freedom? Put God's Words Above All Others!

Again, God sees and does things differently. The Bible says, "For God has not given us a spirit of fear, but of power and of love and of a sound mind" (2 Tim. 1:7, emphasis mine). Freedom comes when we put God's words ahead of and above the words, opinions, and recommendations of everyone else.

The Adam in you might be afraid, but the Christ in you fears nothing! The real-life problem we face is that Adam is still very much with us and we all need to get delivered from him and his ways.

The Bible says, "There is no fear in love; but *perfect love casts out fear...*" (1 John 4:18a, emphasis mine). Fear isn't moved by manipulation, it can only be cast out by love.

God expects each of us to conform to something greater than ourselves and our circumstances: the image of Christ (see Rom. 8:29). The popular culture presses us to conform to the worlds way of doing things.

God says one thing while the old Adam nature screams another. What can we do about it? The Book of James provides the answer:

20   "Therefore lay aside all filthiness and overflow of wickedness, and receive with meekness the implanted word, which is able to save your souls. *But be doers of the word, and not hearers only, deceiving yourselves.* For if anyone is a hearer of the word and not a doer, he is like a man observing his natural face in a mirror; for he observes himself, goes away, and *immediately forgets what kind of man he was.* But he who looks into the perfect law of liberty and continues in it, and is not a forgetful hearer but a doer of the word, this one will be blessed in what he does (Jas. 1:21-25, emphasis mine).

James didn't give us permission to "make exceptions" for people with bad childhoods, an impoverished background, divorced parents, or a bankruptcy petition before the court.

We have God's prescription in hand—will we take it?

Chapter 2

We Have All Been Addicts

Our churches are filled with Christians who are so wounded that they can barely hold their masks in place. Some of us (if not most of us) have allowed ourselves to be victimized. We didn't have to and we didn't' want to, it is just that we didn't know any better.

We have all been addicts of other folks' opinions at one time or another. And anyone who has dealt with addictions will tell you that addiction affects your behavior. It taints your decision-making abilities, corrupts your values, and clouds your thinking.

An addict is defined as one who "devotes or surrenders (oneself) to something habitually or obsessively."[1] It is a "compulsive need for and use of a habit-forming substance…" or "persistent compulsive use of a substance known by the user to be harmful."[2]

It is clear to me that this definition falls short of reality. Addiction goes far beyond mere "substances." We easily become addicted to human approval, gambling, pornography, videogame violence, and countless other non-substances.

A compulsive drive for your addiction can consume your thoughts, invade your dreams, ignite your impulses, and ruthlessly move aside every contender for your attention and focus.

In others words, you feel you have to get a fix everyday. At its worst, this compulsive drive can cause us to fish for, crave, and manipulate people and circumstances to win an "approval hit" everyday from somebody—and sometimes from anybody*!*

Far too often, we don't feel we can ever have a good day if we fail to get our fix. Our happiness literally hinges on the whims and momentary attitudes of other people toward us.

What causes us to hang our happiness on such a flimsy and dangerous thread? What do we do when our addiction becomes our affliction and we lose track of how God defines and establishes a "good day"?

When you truly know God, then every day you wake up is a good day. Things can't do anything but get better. Your happiness isn't anchored on or affected by what kind of news the doctor gives you. Why? Because there is healing inside of you. If God dwells in your heart, then there are blessings inside of you.

We know this is the potential, the possible, the desirable. How do we cross over the line from mere potential to rich reality?

Admit Your Addiction and Confront Your Affliction

Jesus came so that we could have life and have it more abundantly. To enjoy the manifestation of this promise, one of the first things we must do is admit our addiction and confront our affliction. It begins with knowledge—the God-kind-of knowledge.

What is the anatomy of our addiction? How did we become so obsessed with the approval and acceptance of others?

We may be blind to its presence, but the addiction still exists in most of us. We all have certain titles we carry with pride—some official and some unofficial and known only to ourselves.

You may have a certain title such as bishop, chief executive officer, president, or senior something in charge of everybody else; or you may have a great deal of money or no money at all, and be proud of either one.

Wealthy people seek the approval of people who are richer

than they are. On the other hand, people who are barely getting by seek the approval of others who share their difficulty. In many cases, they will do almost anything to avoid their disapproval over "being like those rich folks."

As for me, I had to deal with the question, "What would Eddie Long do if people didn't call me Bishop anymore?" I remember the time I was walking down a hallway at the White House with about 10 other bishops for a scheduled meeting with the President. Somebody said, "Bishop" and all ten of us turned around!

When we entered the room for our meeting with the President, we were wearing nametags that had been carefully prepared in advance by the White House staff. The tags only had *first names* on them.

Suddenly I Noticed I Was "Just Eddie"

We were important people in the hallway, and we all responded when someone called out the title we carried. "Bishop!" When we were in the room with the President of the United States, suddenly I noticed that I was "just Eddie." It was an humbling experience, but now I realize it was good for us.

When the Lord birthed in me this message about the image of Adam, He took me right back to that situation at the White House. Then He spoke to my heart:

> **"Are you really proud of your title? Do you think you are 'all that' because you are a bishop? My covenant did not say I would make your *title* great. If you are living off of an earthly title—whether it is bishop, doctor, president, or CEO—that isn't from Me. I will not make your title great. I promised to you through Abraham that I would bless you and make your *name* great (Gen. 12:2, emphasis mine)."**

24 When we base our identity on an outward title or the earthly approval of people, then as soon as the title or acclaim runs out, so does our reason for living.

People commit suicide or find solace in alcohol, pills, and other addictions when companies "downsize" or when Wall Street's investments take a dip. Desperate people reach for their guns, needles, or comfort foods the moment a relationship goes sour or a foreclosure notice arrives in the mail.

Why? Because their entire self-identity is based on sand. They believe their future hangs in the balance because of their money problems, a layoff notice, a demotion, or because someone snubbed them at work or at church.

Are You "In Christ" or "In Your Title"?

Jesus described two foundations available to every one of us:

> "Therefore whoever hears these sayings of Mine, and does them, I will liken him to a wise man *who built his house on the rock:* and the rain descended, the floods came, and the winds blew and beat on that house; and it did not fall, for it was founded on the rock. But everyone who hears these sayings of Mine, and does not do them, will be like a foolish man *who built his house on the sand:* and the rain descended, the floods came, and the winds blew and beat on that house; and it fell. And great was its fall" (Mt. 7:24-27, emphasis mine)

Are you in Christ or *in your title?* Do you live by what God says or by what people say? That is why we have so many insecure people in the Body of Christ. They quickly get upset if someone says, "Well, they might be moving you out of your position soon...."

The truth is that when you are i*n Christ, the Second Adam,* you can never be moved out of your "position." Why? Because you can say with Paul and every other *Believer* in Jesus Christ:

> *"My God has made me alive together with Christ (by grace I have been saved), and raised us up together, and made us sit together in the heavenly places in Christ Jesus. We are seated together high above principality. It doesn't have anything to do with boardrooms, economic indicators, opinion polls, or layoff notices. It has all to do with my position in Christ"* (adapted in part from Eph. 1:20-21, 2:5-6).

Too Much of the World and Too Little of Christ

Why don't we live this way in real life? Because we have all been addicts, and most of us are still struggling with our crippling addiction. We have too much of the world and too little of Christ in us.

We take after the garden-variety Adam, our earthly great granddaddy in the flesh. When the first Adam disobeyed God's direct command, he abandoned his identity as God's highest creation. He was made "in the image and likeness of God" and yet he chose the serpent's way.

Adam and Eve chose to be *separate* from their Maker so they could possess "the knowledge of good and evil." Unfortunately, the holy and divine part of their identity died the day they abandoned God.

Philosophers, religious leaders, and (in later years) psychologists have attempted to justify and describe life without God, and came up with terms such as ego, alter ego, the ego ideal, the super ego, the id, and countless other terms and concepts. It may still be reduced to one common denominator: life apart from God.

We are born as heirs of the first Adam who is spiritually dead and separated from God. When we repent and are reborn through Jesus Christ, the Second Adam dwells in us as the life-giving Spirit of God.

Members of the human race have struggled since the fall in Genesis to develop words, ways, and religious concepts explaining why we exist, why there is a void in the human psyche, and why we don't need God to be fulfilled. Popular American talk show hosts, feel-good psychologists, and self-help gurus talk constantly about a healthy ego or self-image.

Your Ego is Not Who You Are

The truth is that your *ego is not who you are.* If you're not careful, you might swallow the world's continuous propaganda campaign and believe your ego or self-image is really you. Your ego or self-image is merely an elaborate social mask, but we've been led to believe that we must never leave home without it.

Have you ever been afraid to look into the eyes of another person? Were you afraid of what they might see? Were you trying to hide behind an invisible mask?

The old Adam nature in us hides behind a carefully prepared self-image. It represents the false picture of what we think we really are to the outside world. The problem is that if the false mask you call "ego" is hurt through rejection, disappointment, or betrayal, then you think you've been hurt. No, that image isn't the real you.

People are often offended, hurt or even perplexed when they find out the truth about themselves. Here is an extreme example: say a young woman who can't stay on pitch to save her life actually believes she is a great singer with genuinely professional potential.

Throughout her life, friends and family have perpetuated the myth with exaggerated compliments and flattering predictions, so in her mind she has an inward conviction with some outward supporting evidence to support her ego, her false self image.

Shattering the Carefully Constructed Mask of Myth   27

Her world collapses when someone finally says, "I'm sorry, but we can't use you. Your voice is pretty but you sing out of tune. It is hopeless." In tears, she sputters, "You hurt me." In reality, all the honest critic did was speak true words that shattered her carefully constructed mask of myth.

"But you don't understand, Bishop. Those people really hurt me."

No, that tells me that you thought a lot of yourself. Understand this: *Other people can only hurt you to the level of your selfishness.*

"How am I selfish?"

When someone says or does something that doesn't agree with your contrived self-image, you get offended and declare that you (which is really your self-image) are hurt. That is why it is so hard to preach the Word of God to the average congregation without compromise.

Every time I preach about sin, or when I describe how the Gentiles (whom the Jews called dogs in Jesus' day) were adopted into God's Kingdom through the blood of Jesus and the cross, people get offended and make comments such as: "I don't like the way Bishop preaches. Sometime I don't like the words he uses. Why, he called us dogs the other day. Now that hurt me."

Many of Our Problems Stem From Wounded Egos

Too many people in the church want preachers and church leaders to anoint them with oil and pray for God's blessings on their lives when many of their problems stem from their wounded egos! The prayer of faith won't help much when you base everything you feel and do in life on what other people say and on the constantly changing circumstances of life.

God did not create us to live that way. He knew from the beginning that bad things would happen to good people at times. That is why He sent His only Son to the cross.

28   It is because of the cross that the Second Adam can live inside of you and me. God's Spirit can explode through every scripture you have stored in your heart and mind. Tangible power flows into our daily lives through verses and divine promises such as:

> "He who is in you is greater than he who is in the world" (1 Jn. 4:4b)

> "I have been crucified with Christ; *it is no longer I who live, but Christ lives in me;* and the life which I now live in the flesh I live by faith in the Son of God, who loved me and gave Himself for me" (Gal. 2:20, emphasis mine).

How is someone going to hurt you when God lives inside you? All they can do is offend the person you pretend to be. If I can say something about who you are pretending to be and I get you upset, then it means you aren't really sure who you are.

We aren't led by the Spirit. The Bible says:

> "For if you live according to the flesh you will die; but if by the Spirit you put to death the deeds of the body, you will live. For as many as are *led by the Spirit of God,* these are sons of God" (Rom. 8:13-14, emphasis mine).

When we are not led by the Spirit of God, then we are led by our addictions, driven by our afflictions, and seduced by our adversary, the devil. How else does the Lord lead us through and protect us in "the valley of the shadow of death" that David talked about (see Ps. 23:4)?

To be honest, most of us act more like addicts under compulsion than like overcomers in Christ. We aren't led by the Spirit. We stumble through at the mercy of our flesh or something worse.

When we aren't totally defeated and pouting in our church services, we are singing and shouting until we get hoarse in the sanctuary (and we may even run up and down the aisle for good measure).

The Test of the Flesh: Pass or Fail?

Then comes the test of the flesh. Somebody pulls in front of us in the church parking lot or accidentally fails to open a door for us; and our flesh comes charging through the false faces we are wearing. "That no-good so and so; who does he think he is?... She walked right by me and didn't speak to me! The nerve. I'm not going back to that church!"

In another place, Paul put it this way:

> "For all the law is fulfilled in one word, even in this: 'You shall love your neighbor as yourself.' But if you bite and devour one another, beware lest you be consumed by one another! I say then: *Walk in the Spirit, and you shall not fulfill the lust of the flesh*" (Gal. 5:14-16, emphasis mine).

Are you a closet addict with a secret compulsion to win the approval of others? I'm convinced we all are at different times and in different ways. And I know God has a better way.

When we live life striving for approval, we want control. We hope to be sustained or held up by our own power or control over people, things, and situations. We dress to impress, swagger to intimidate, flirt to capture attention, and give gifts to win favor. We avoid known problems and target the easily solved ones; and we may even put down or downgrade the virtues of others to win favor for ourselves.

Imagine a Life of Freedom

Why do we struggle to accumulate power, influence, and

approval at home, at work, and in the church? It is because we live in fear.

Imagine for a moment what it would be like to live in freedom and not be influenced by other folks' opinions; to have joy and experience a "good day" even when difficult things happen. Can you imagine what it would be like to live that way? That is the life that Christ wants you to live!

Every once in awhile you run across some cool saints who don't care about what you say—they love you anyway. They don't care about the approval or disapproval of Deacon Critical and Presbyter Sister Shine On. They are in Christ and His opinion has risen above all others in importance and influence over their lives.

When you are in Christ, you aren't trying to control everything and everyone around you. You know your destiny, and you realize that you can't be stopped or hindered unless you step out of God's will.

Now people who have escaped their addiction to man's opinion act differently from other people. Even if you say things that were crafted to hurt and discourage them, they are content to just let you run on and on.

> *You may say, "Child, you know they're laying people off at the factory. You better be careful."*
>
> *In turn they respond, "They might be laying people off but I'm not worried about it, because I know my destiny. I know who God is, and my future is not determined by outside circumstances. Each day of my life is determined by what God has placed in me. And He who has begun a good work in me shall complete it! My destiny is not determined by the economy or by every Wall Street hiccup or White House mixup."*

Are You Immune to Criticism and Flattery?   **31**
(Would You Like to Be?)

Most of us are far too busy trying to be something other people want or expect us to be. Those who really are led by the Spirit in the Last Adam are immune to criticism and flattery (but are very open to godly correction). They have no fear because they know God is with them. Whatever comes up is all right because the One inside them knew the things that would occur in their lives, and He has already worked it out.

People struggling with addictive behavior need someone who will hold them accountable for their actions and remind them of the steps to freedom. They need someone who knows what comes next in the cycle of breaking free from compulsion. They need someone who will never, ever give up.

The bad news is that we have all been addicts. The Good News is that we have a Savior who never fails.

We don't have to fear the future because we serve the God who knows the end from the beginning (see Isa. 46:10). All we've got to do is continue to get up and keep moving, regardless of circumstances.

Facing the Fears of Discovery and Depravation

The greatest fears of an addict include the fear of discovery, of being found out; and the fear of depravation, the fear that the object and source of their addiction—whether it be crystal methamphetamine, crack cocaine, alcohol, or the approval of others—may somehow be taken from them.

It is time for us to face our fears. We have already been "found out." Our addiction to the approval of others is a matter of public record, and the cure for our affliction is only a choice away. Once we choose to be free, God acts on our behalf.

What if God leaves me? That would be a problem if it were a possibility, but it isn't. He promised us:

"Peace I leave with you, My peace I give to you; not as the world gives do I give to you. Let not your heart be troubled, neither let it be afraid" (John 14:27).

For He Himself has said, *"I will never leave you nor forsake you."* So we may boldly say: "The Lord is my helper; I will not fear. What can man do to me?" (Heb. 13:5b-6, emphasis mine).

Deliverance from addiction may lead to another set of problems for the unwary and the unwise.

The Scriptures tell us that a man named Jacob who was addicted to man's approval and to a lifestyle of deceit and deception was delivered from his affliction—but he was left with a limp the rest of his life (see Gen. 32).

Jacob was renamed Israel by the Lord, but he limped for the rest of his life. It was a permanent reminder of his moment of transformation. Pride is perhaps a Christian's most dangerous enemy.

The Last Adam Walks in Humility, Not Superiority

If you are walking in the Second Adam (the Last Adam, which is the Spirit of Christ), you should walk in a degree of humility and feel confident, yet superior to no one.

A mature Christian who has been delivered from the compulsion to control and win approval from others recognizes that everyone else in the Kingdom is of the same spirit, though they may have different "disguises" or outward appearances.

Whether you serve faithfully in a ministry to the poor, drive a bus to pickup children for church services, pastor a church, or serve as a bishop leading many churches, you are valuable in God's sight. Just because I serve in the capacity of bishop does not make me better than you; nor does it authorize me to lord over you.

We are what we are strictly by God's mercy and grace—the **33** only part we play in this Kingdom drama is in our obedience to His will. God doesn't have any "big I's" and "little you's."

God's Spirit constantly works in our hearts to deliver us and steer us clear of Adam's ego-based power. Before I preached the first message in this series on the two Adams, I had worked for four hours on a major message. When I finally finished it, the Lord told me to put it down, and then He gave me the core message on "Deliver Me From Adam."

"I'm Going To Make You Humble"

He said to my spirit, "I am going to make you humble before you preach this." He wasn't kidding. I had to stand and preach what I had at that moment, openly confessing to the people that I was still wrestling with the issues it raised, and that I didn't know where it would take me in the end.

The Lord said, "If you operate in this ego-based power of the first Adam stage, it will only last as long as the object of reference is there. As soon as the title or the job or the money goes away, so does the power."

On the other hand, walking in the Spirit with the Last Adam, Jesus Christ, is permanent. Why? Because it is based on the knowledge of Him. Paul described it perfectly:

"Therefore, if anyone is [out of Adam and] in Christ, he is a new creation; old things have passed away; behold, all things have become new" (2 Cor. 5:17, **emphasis and parenthetical insertions mine**).

We tend to misunderstand and misquote this scripture at times. We say, "Therefore, if any man be in Christ, he is a new creature, old habits pass away, old stuff that I used to do...." That isn't quite true.

Remember, your ego isn't you. Your ego is part of the first

34 Adam's self-identity. Our desperate attempts to protect that false approval-seeking identity are just an outward show and a joke. Any effort to protect this false identity and mask may keep you from being in Christ.

Is Your Old Man too Busy to Die?

As long as a person can offend you (the false you who is desperate to please others), then the "old Adam you" will never die. Why? Your "old man" is too busy to die—it is consumed with being hurt and offended and trying to get somebody back.

The old must die before the new can live. The pattern appears in the very beginning, in the Garden of Eden, where so many other things were established and foreshadowed. As we read earlier:

> **"And so it is written, The *last Adam* became a life-giving spirit. However, *the spiritual is not first, but the natural,* and afterward the spiritual. *The first man was of the earth, made of dust...* " (1 Cor. 15:45-47a, emphasis mine).**

Paul is describing the Garden Adam, the prototype model. God our Creator didn't create Adam's spirit and then craft a body for him to possess. It happened the other way around.

First, God made Adam's body from the dust of the earth. Then He *breathed* on the clay form He had made. First the natural; then the spiritual. Adam lost his true identity because he lost sight of his true reason for existence.

We regain our true selves in Christ by allowing the natural Adam to die. What Jesus completed at the "tree" on Calvary actually began in the beginning at another tree. We must revisit the Garden to rediscover our reason for being.

End Notes

1. *Merriam Webster's Collegiate Dictionary, Tenth Edition* (Springfield, MA: Merriam-Webster, Inc., 1994), p. 13, adapted from the definition for the verb transitive form of "addict."

2. Ibid, from the definition for the noun, "addiction."

Chapter 3
Finding Out Why You Are Here

You can run but you can't hide: Finding out your purpose in life is important. If you don't, then every passing slam or criticism about your value or existence will strike home as something that just might be true.

Insults lose their power to wound and destroy you when you know *who* you are and *Whose* you are. You just won't care about cutting comments and wounding words if you know the reality of God and why He created us.

Our modern western culture tends to avoid questions about why we are here. The subject is too serious for a popular culture known better for its beer commercials than for its search for the true meaning of life.

This is the situation: Adam's problems began only after he forgot why he was created and placed in the Garden. The human family has struggled with that curse ever since Adam's decision from the dawn of time.

Now the problem has landed in our laps. We have to go back to God – the Source of our existence.

"...**He gives to all life, breath, and all things. And He has made from one blood every nation of men to dwell on all the face of the earth, and has determined their preappointed times...**so *that they should seek the Lord,* **in the hope that they might grope for Him and find Him, though He is not far from each one of us;** *for in Him we live and move and have our being,* **as also some of your own poets have said, 'For we are also His offspring'"** (Acts 17:25-28, emphasis mine).

When Adam and Eve disobeyed God and took the serpent's bait, they discarded God's image and likeness in favor of their own self-image. The decision to find self value – separate from God their Creator – introduced death into their destiny (and ours).

Death wasn't there until that moment of decision in the Garden, but it plagues us to this day. When we live in the first Adam, we think we're hurt when somebody messes with our ego, but the "real us" is hidden in Christ. This false "you" is a self-manufactured image of who you think you should be based on the opinions and actions of other people.

Playing a Part on the Stage of Life

Life in the first Adam promotes a life of hypocrisy, a word that originally referred to "the act of playing a part on the stage...a feigning to be what one is not."[1]

Ego (or what we now call the ego) is at the heart of this act.[2] It is a false mask that leads most of us around throughout life, bouncing us from one offense, rejection or shortcoming to the next, and artificially boosting us from one concocted reality to the next as circumstances dictate.

As we noted earlier, Jesus said, "I have come that they (those who believe) may have life, and that they may have it *more abundantly*" (John 10:10b, emphasis mine). He wasn't playing around; He meant what He said.

You have to find out why you are here! Once you discover your reason for existence and begin to work and move in that destiny, it will bring you joy. That is good news! Nehemiah 8:10 says, "...the joy of the Lord is your strength."

Life Is More Than Getting and Hoarding Stuff

Americans are taught from their earliest days that life consists of doing stuff, possessing stuff, getting more stuff through personal effort, and receiving even more stuff from other people. All of that happens in life, but there is *more* to life than getting and hoarding "stuff."

Jesus boiled everything down to a single choice for two ladies who were very close to Him.

> "Now it happened as they went that He entered a certain village; and a certain woman named Martha welcomed Him into her house. And she had a sister called Mary, who also sat at Jesus' feet and heard His word. But Martha was distracted with much serving, and she approached Him and said, 'Lord, do You not care that my sister has left me to serve alone? Therefore tell her to help me.' And Jesus answered and said to her, 'Martha, Martha, you are worried and troubled about many things. But one thing is *needed,* and Mary has *chosen* that good part, which will not be taken away from her'" (Luke 10:38-42, emphasis mine).

Mary made the best choice and it moved her closer to her destiny. Paul said, "All things were created through [Jesus Christ] and for Him" (Col. 1:16b).

John wrote in the Book of Revelation: "You are worthy, O Lord, to receive glory and honor and power; for You created all things, and by Your will [for thy pleasure—KJV] they exist and were created" (Rev. 4:11, emphasis mine).

You and I were created for God's pleasure. He loves us, He enjoys spending time with us, and He especially enjoys the praise and worship we offer Him.

Has Life Become Dreadful and Heavy?

According to Jesus, "But the hour is coming, and now is, when the true worshippers will worship the Father in spirit and truth; for the Father is seeking such to worship Him" (John 4:23, emphasis mine).

For too many of us, life has become a dread, a weight, and a big mess because we have become tied up in things that have nothing to do with who we are and what we are about.

Wake up and live! All you have to work with is now. Don't be "planning" to live in some future day in your imagination. Live *right now!*

Members of my congregation still remember the Sunday we heard inspiring testimonies about God's faithfulness, and I told everyone to "go home and party." It was a great day of celebration, and you could hear people telling one another, "I hope Bishop preaches that sermon again so we can party again."

My question is this: "Why don't we make it a lifestyle? We should celebrate God's faithfulness every day!" Whether people say it aloud or not, the answer they are really thinking usually goes like this: "Well, you know, Bishop, everything isn't the way I want it now."

What is my response? "Well things aren't as bad as they could be, so you should just celebrate what you are, where you are, and who you are in Christ right now!" It is time to live.

If you steep your life at godless sites on the Internet, or in popular situation comedies, MTV, BET specials, or the evening news, then you are investing precious hours into things that can pull you away from your true reason for living.

The popular media, entertainment, and cultural influences tend to place all focus on "me," and they do it from a twisted viewpoint. The goal is for your "me" to be conformed to views, values, and tastes of others. This may include those of leading advertisers, entertainers, marketing experts, and powerful opinion brokers in the political and economic realms. Such is life under twisted influence....

> *It is easy to influence the actions of people*
> *who don't know who they are, why they*
> *exist, or where they are going.*

The power of peer pressure is brought to bear on all of us, **41** influencing us to wear the politically correct or most fashionable clothes, drink the right beverages, wear the right athletic shoes, drive the right cars, attend the right schools, and hold the politically correct opinions about morals, politics, and religious expressions (virtually no expression is acceptable if you are a born-again Christian).

Our teens are bombarded with pressure-packed messages encouraging sexual promiscuity, alcohol use, and everything else that goes into "fitting in with the crowd."

What happens when your true self—your spirit in Christ— is completely free of those things? Look at it from the non-Christian's viewpoint: What do you do with people who have a heavenly mandate to *take over* their world using nothing but the force of love and Christ-centered righteousness? You defeat them (impossible), you join them (desirable), or you just get out of the way.

It is easy to influence the actions of people who don't know who they are, why they exist, or where they are going. On the other hand, it is very difficult to manipulate people who have a genuine love relationship with God.

Living In the Unbreakable Bond of Unconditional Love

God wants us to live in an unbreakable bond of unconditional love, with a clear-cut understanding of our divine destiny and mission in life!

For much of the time when the Holy Spirit was birthing this book in my life, I was preaching ahead of what I had actually experienced and assimilated in my heart. I thought I had already absorbed the truth of Genesis 1:26.

This is the passage where God said, "Let us make man in our *image,* according to our *likeness;* let them have *dominion* over the fish of the sea, over the birds of the air, and over the cattle, over all the earth and over every creeping thing that creeps on the earth."

42   The next two verses tell us twice that God created us in His image. They also say that He created us male and female, that He blessed us, and that He commanded us to *"Be fruitful and multiply; fill the earth and subdue it; have dominion* over the fish of the sea, and *over every living thing* that moves on the earth"* (Gen. 1:28).

All of these verses describe life in the Garden before the curse. We know that Adam and Eve fell into sin through their choice to be separate from their Creator. Look again at Paul's summary of our predicament:

> **"For as *in Adam* all die, even so i*n Christ all* shall be made alive... . And so it is written, 'The first man Adam became a living being.' The last Adam became a *life-giving spirit"* (1 Cor. 15:22, 45, emphasis mine).**

Do You Merely Exist For the Purpose of Dying?

When you continue to exist in Adam, then you merely exist for the purpose of dying. When you live in Christ, you become a life-giving spirit with a destiny of eternal life in the presence of God. If you are not alive, then you cannot give life.

The Bible says something amazing about faces, masks, and freedom:

> **"Now the Lord is the Spirit; and where the Spirit of the Lord is, there is liberty. But we all, with unveiled face, beholding as in a mirror the glory of the Lord, are being transformed into the same image from glory to glory, just as by the Spirit of the Lord" (2 Cor 3:17-18, emphasis mine).**

When I examined the literal meanings of the Greek term for "liberty" that Paul used in this verse, I discovered some powerful facts:[3]

1. The liberty you and I receive from the Spirit of the Lord means we are unrestrained by Adam's fatal decision in the Garden. The chains of his curse are removed from our spirits, minds, and bodies.

2. We are free to live as citizens of God's Kingdom, not slaves of His fallen angel, or as slaves to Adam's sin.

3. We are literally exempt from every obligation or liability incurred by the sin of Adam and Eve and the judgment they received for it.

Something Amazing Happens To Our Masks...

When we live our lives in the first Adam, we create elaborate masks to put up a false front of who we think we are or should be. Paul showed us that something amazing happens to our masks when we live in Christ. This has everything to do with understanding why we are here on earth. The original Greek meanings for "open face" reveal that:

1. **Something is *taken away or reversed* when we step into the liberty of the Spirit of the Lord.[4]**

2. **Our false Adam masks, the "false fronts" we present to the world, are simply removed and their need is reversed by God's freedom.[5]**

All of this comes about as we focus on the Lord's face by "beholding as in a mirror the glory of the Lord," rather than on our makeshift social masks, our egos, or the opinions of others.

Do you know why you are here? Are you here to die, or are you living and breathing to live supernaturally and reflect God's glory and divine purpose on the earth?

Separated or Inseparable From the Creator

Will you live and die separated from your Creator and your purpose for living, or will you live eternally inseparable from your Creator and your divine purpose?

The answer will make all the difference in the way you live your lives, make your decisions, and plan your days.

When Jesus taught the Disciples how to pray, He planted the Father's divine plan right at the heart of the perfect prayer model:

"**In this manner, therefore, pray: Our Father in heaven, hallowed be Your name.** *Your Kingdom come. Your will be done on earth* **as it is in heaven. Give us this day our daily bread. And forgive us our debts, as we forgive our debtors. And do not lead us into temptation, but deliver us from the evil one. For yours is the Kingdom and the power and the glory forever. Amen"** (Mt. 6:9-13, emphasis mine).

This is a perfect restatement of Adam's original mandate before his fatal sin. We were created to love God, to glorify Him, and to *exercise dominion* over His creation in His name and authority. In other words, God's Kingdom and those who belong to it are supposed to rule or *take over.*

Before we entered the new millennium, I described my vision of the overcoming church that would arise in this century in a book titled, *Taking Over: Seizing Your City for God in the New Millennium.*

These statements about the church also apply to you, specifically as you discover who you really are and why you are here:

When the house of God, the church, sets itself in order according to God's Word, it will operate in supernatural power, vision, and authority as never before. The true church, the separated church, has every solution the world needs. We have the authority and supernatural wisdom needed to right society's wrongs and bring order wherever there is chaos, but it all begins at the cross.

We are not called to link arms with everybody and every organization that comes along with a good cause. Let them link arms with us after they lay aside their private agendas and alliances with devils, for we have something far superior to any good cause or noble end. We are the people of God; we carry the Spirit of the Savior and the power of the Creator. We serve the Lamb of God who takes away the sins of the world. We come in the name of the King of kings and the Lord of lords, not merely in the name of a good cause or some nice idea.[6]

You Gotta Know Why You Are Here!

Sometimes I just have to deviate from standard English to get across the importance of a statement, and this is one of those times: You gotta know why you are here! Your future depends on it!

The Bible says, "Where the Spirit of the Lord is, there is liberty?" (2 Cor. 3:17) and "...with the mouth, confession is made unto salvation" (Rom. 10:10b). Say this out loud:

I am completely free. Even if others don't approve of me or my decision to live *in Christ,* I am *still* free. Their disapproval doesn't bother me or change my course.

If you refuse to speak affirming words to me and you withhold your approval or support, I am *still* free.

If danger invades my neighborhood or surrounds me with threats, and if others fall victim to fear or desperation over the economy, terrorism, or health challenges, I am still free and unmoved by circumstances.

I am not anchored in my own strength or wisdom. My hope is in the one who keeps me and watches over me day and night. I know that "if God be for us, who can be against us?" (see Rom. 8:31b).

I cannot be denied; I cannot be torn down. I was choosen by God to complete a specific mission. He is the One who gave me life. He preserves my health and gives me the power to get wealth. He is my strong tower and my glory, and the lifter of my head.

God is not like us—He always finishes what He begins. He began a good work in me, and I know that He will finish it. I am positioned to fulfill my destiny. I refuse to back up or lay down. I was born to rule and take over in Jesus' name and image.

Live As An Eternal Being With a Divine Destiny

We enter this world from the womb and gradually become aware of the tomb awaiting us at the other *end* of human life. That brings us to a choice: we can pretend it won't happen and live like the devil or look to our Creator, discover why He gave us life, and live each day as eternal beings with a divine destiny.

You gotta know why you are here!

God brought you into this world and when He gets ready, He will take you out of it to be with Him. He created you to live in freedom through Christ, and He called and anointed you to rule and reign as an heir with Jesus.

Aren't you tired of living like a slave and worrying about the death sentence handed down to you through the first Adam? You've been adopted by the King and given an eternal inheritance. It is time to live like royalty and walk with authority. Now take your place among God's chosen and begin to live and take dominion in freedom!

1. *Merriam Webster's Collegiate Dictionary, Tenth Edition,* p. 571, from the etymology and definition for "hypocrisy."

2. Where they appear in this book, I reluctantly borrow from terminology popular in North American culture originating with the psychoanalytic theories of Sigmund Freud. Much of his work is in direct opposition to the truths and concepts of God's Word, and therefore must be largely set aside or carefully limited in use. I may use terms such as *ego* (the supposed organized conscious that mediates between the person and the reality of the outside world—perceiving and adapting to it), *superego* (supposedly a partially conscious part of personality that holds the "internalized" values of parents, society, and experience; and rewards or punishes through a series of moral views, guilt, and conscience), and *id* (supposedly the subconscious part of personality that drives and energizes the psyche, and is rooted in instinctual drives and needs). However, I do *not* agree with them in totality, but their use where necessary may help readers revise their views to conform to God's view of our true design and makeup as revealed in the Bible.

3. James Strong, *Strong's Exhaustive Concordance of the Bible* (Peabody, MA: Hendrickson Publishers, n.d.), "liberty," Greek, el-yoo-ther-ee'ah; from G1658; *freedom* (legitimate or licentious, chiefly mor. or cer.):–liberty. 1658. eleutheros, el-yoo'-ther-os; prob. from the alt. of G2064; *unrestrained* (to go at pleasure), i.e. (as a citizen) *not a slave* (whether freeborn or manumitted), or (gen.) *exempt (from obligation or liability):* –free (man, woman), at liberty. NOTE: I italicized portions of these quoted definitions (and those that follow) to point out the sources for my comments in the text.

4. *Strong, Strong's Exhaustive Concordance of the Bible,* "open or unveiled," Greek, 343, anakalupto, an-ak-al-oop'-to; from G303 *(in the sense of reversal)* and G2572; *to unveil:* –open, ([un-]) *taken away.*

5. Ibid, "face," Greek: 4383. prosopon, pros'-o-pon; from

48 G4314 and ops *(the visage; from G3700); the front* (as being towards view), i.e. the countenance, aspect, appearance, surface; by impl. presence, person:–(outward) appearance, before, countenance, face, fashion, (men's) person, presence.

6. Eddie Long, *Taking Over: Seizing Your City for God in the New Millenium* (Lake Mary, FL: Creation House, 1999), 154.

Chapter 4
The Image of True Authority

God said from the beginning, "Let them have dominion." Unfortunately, *we don't.*

Are you tired of reading scriptures that you cannot live and believing for miracles that you do not see? Some of us act and think as if the Bible is just a storybook of things that happened long ago.

Let me say it straight. Subconsciously, many Christians believe God is dead. It amazes me to see how loud we'll shout about it and then go home and doubt it!

"How can you say that, Bishop? Of course we believe God is alive."

We were "in Adam" before we began to be "in Christ." Yet, even now we doubt God's Word because we rarely walk in and do His Word. We live in Adam's world so we have trouble walking in Christ's authority.

That is why the Apostle Paul explained that when we were children concerning spiritual things, we spoke as children and acted like children. Then he put a big "but" in the middle of it all: "...but when I became a man, I put away childish things. For now we see in a mirror, dimly, but then face to face. Now I know in part, but then I shall know just as I also am known" (1 Cor. 13:11b-12).

That means I have to put away all the "Adam stuff" I learned and inherited. For me to live, I have to walk as Christ—the last Adam—walked.

God challenges us to fulfill His original mandate from Genesis 1:26: "Let us make man in our image, according to

50 our likeness; let them have dominion over the fish of the sea, over the birds of the air."

What Is Your Image?

Christian maturity is all about image. Whose image do we bear, and what authority does it carry? During the astrology craze of the 60's, the common cliché throughout our culture was, "What's your sign?" God asks another question that is neither cliché nor outdated: "What is your image?"

One night my wife and I were watching television in our bedroom when we heard the unmistakable evidence of "problems" coming from the upstairs bedroom temporarily occupied by my son and daughter. The bedroom is far enough away from us that if we could hear anything at all, then that meant a lot was going on.

We heard the noise over the sounds of our TV program, and some of the louder thumps seemed to go through the whole house. At that point, my wife looked at me and said, "You need to go investigate."

As an experienced father, I knew enough to walk softly as I climbed the stairs and rounded the corner. The volume rose with each step, and I was amazed by what I heard. It sounded as if objects of various sizes were being thrown as my two unsuspecting kids fussed at each other and fought things out. (I know you assumed that my household is perfect, but the truth will set you free.)

Neither of them heard me nor saw me coming, so it was a total surprise when I walked into Taylor's room. They were acting crazy, doing silly stuff, and being just as loud as they could possibly be—before I entered the room.

Then I turned the corner, and they saw me. They stopped instantly—even though I didn't say anything. In other words, the lawlessness stopped the moment I showed up.

The Image of Authority Walked In

What quieted the noise in our upstairs bedroom? Why did the problem suddenly cease to exist? It happened because the *image of authority* walked on the scene.

We are called and anointed to walk in God's image of authority all the time, but we seem to exhibit signs of spiritual dyslexia at times. We get the proper order or sequence of things backwards. We want dessert before supper, the paycheck before the labor, the intimacy before the marriage, and the dominion before the image.

God hasn't changed...He is still the God of order. He did not say, "Let them have dominion...okay, now I create them in My image." No, God said:

"Let us make man i*n our image, according to our likeness;* let them have dominion over the fish of the sea, over the birds of the air, and over the cattle, over all the earth and over every creeping thing that creeps on the earth" (Gen 1:26, emphasis mine).

First, it's the image and likeness; then the dominion. He is saying, essentially, "If you operate like me, if you look like me, then you automatically have what I have. You don't have to 'buff it up' or put on a muscle tee shirt, and you don't need a special license plate. You don't need anything on the outside, because what you are is Me!"

Mostly Talk With Very Little Walk

God wants to take us to a higher place where we conduct spiritual warfare without saying, "I bind you...." I am convinced that the reason we have to say so much in our efforts to conduct spiritual warfare is because we are "not that much."

We are mostly talk with very little walk. In fact, I'm concerned that many in the modern church come far too close to matching the picture of the questionable saints Jesus painted in Matthew 7:

> *"Therefore by their fruits you will know them.* **Not everyone who says to Me, 'Lord, Lord,' shall enter the Kingdom of heaven, but he who does the will of my Father in heaven. Many will say to me in that day, 'Lord, Lord, have we not prophesied in Your name, cast out demons in Your name, and done many wonders in Your name?' And then I will declare to them,** *'I never knew you; depart from Me,* **you who practice lawlessness!"** (Matthew 7: 20-23, emphasis mine).

Basically, Jesus was saying, "My name will do a whole lot of stuff. In fact, My name will do everything. But that does not mean that you are operating in what I ordained for you. If you were operating in the things I ordained for you, then you wouldn't even have to say my name...because you would begin to bear My image and walk in My authority."

People Call Them When Trouble Comes

There are a number of people in my congregation who are frequently called when other people get in trouble. Sometimes a relative has gotten drunk or high, or a fight is about to break out at someone's house.

When the person who's walking in the Spirit shows up, things have a way of calming down. Why? Because of the image or presence they display. They don't have to say much because the image of *God* shows through them with divine authority.

This should give us a hint about the principles revealed in God's Word where Paul declares:

"Therefore God also has highly exalted Him and given Him the name which is above every name, that at the *name of Jesus* every knee should bow, of those in heaven, and of those on earth, and of those under the earth, and that every tongue should confess that Jesus Christ is Lord, to the glory of God the Father" (Phil. 2:9-11, emphasis mine).

If the power of Jesus Christ could be released by merely mentioning His name, then everyone could tap it—including Satan. The Greek word translated as "name" in this verse means much, much more.

According to *Strong's Exhaustive Concordance of the Bible,* the Greek word for "name" refers literally to Jesus' authority and *character.*[2]

This word *(onoma)* is used "for all that a name implies, of authority, character, rank, majesty, power, excellence, etc., of everything that the name covers."[3]

It does not mean that you have to say it, but rather that you have to *BE* it. When you actually begin to walk in God's image, you have the power of God's image.

It is God Who Works in You

How does it work? Paul explained it in simple terms when he wrote, "For *it is God* who works *in you* both to will and to do for His good pleasure" (Phil. 2:13, emphasis mine).

Most of us don't walk in the divine favor God ordained for us because we don't walk in His image. Instead we stumble through life carrying a badly modified version of Adam's old image. This self-made remake was bad to begin with, and when we adapt it in response to the ever-changing opinions of others, things go from bad to worse. God wants us to have something far better.

The typical churchgoer might find comfort in the thought: "Well, I'm messed up and I'll be messed up until Jesus comes, but at least I'm created in the image of God."

I'm sorry, but does your life agree with the second part of that statement? Once again, compare this popular statement with God's unchanging word:

> **"This is the book of the genealogy of Adam. In the day that God created man, He made him in the likeness of God. He created them male and female, and blessed them and called them Mankind in the day they were created. And Adam lived one hundred and thirty years, and begot a son in his own likeness, after his image, and named him Seth" (Gen. 5:1-3).**

Most Are More Like Adam Than Like God

This is Adam's likeness and image—not God's. That means we have a serious problem: most of us are more like Adam than like God. We have not made the transformation from having the image of the first Adam to walking in the image of the last Adam, Jesus Christ. This is why we should cry, "Lord deliver me from Adam!"

According to *Vines Expository Dictionary of Old and New Testament Words,* the Hebrew word translated as "image" in Genesis 1:26 means "a copy or counterpart."[4] That means God created us as an earthly carbon copy and counterpart.

When Adam and Eve chose to believe the serpent's lies and disobey God's direct command, they changed images becoming second-hand copies of the first fallen angel rather than of God the creator.

In God's mercy, He sent His Son to die on the cross and restore our original image and likeness. Now, we have the unique privilege of "putting on Christ" in this life and not just "the sweet bye and bye" of heaven.

"For you are all sons of God through faith in Christ
Jesus. For as many of you as were *baptized* into Christ
have *put on Christ.* There is neither Jew nor Greek,
there is neither slave nor free, there is neither male nor
female; for you are *all one in Christ Jesus.* And if you are
Christ's, then you are Abraham's seed, and heirs according to the promise" (Gal. 3: 26-29, emphasis mine).

Through the cross, Jesus Christ removed everything that
separates us from Him and divides us from one another.
If anything still divides us, it is because we continue to cling
to the old and refuse the new Adam's image—not because
God failed to take care of our image problem.

When God Breaks Out

God's image isn't some lacquer coating or thin veneer that
you brush or glue on the outside. It is a supernatural power
source you carry around inside you. You open your mouth,
look with your eyes, touch with your hands, or even enter a
room and God breaks out.

". . . the mystery…has been hidden from ages and
from generations, but now has been revealed to His
saints. To them God willed to make known what are the
riches of the glory of this mystery among the Gentiles:
which is *Christ in you, the hope of glory.* Him we preach,
warning every man and teaching every man in all
wisdom, that we may present every man *perfect
in Christ Jesus"* (Col. 1: 26-28, emphasis mine).

Once again, it all boils down to this: "For as in Adam
all die, (say all die) even so in Christ all shall be made alive…
And so it is written, 'The first man Adam became a living
being.' The last Adam became a life-giving spirit." (1 Cor.
15:22, 45).

We usually won't walk in the image of true authority until we've paid the price in commitment and total surrender to the new Adam way of life. It reminds me of what happens to a new recruit who joins the U.S. Armed Forces.

Transformation is the Fruit of Transition

New recruits often enter the service with grand ideas of wearing an officer's uniform, flying an aircraft, navigating a submarine under arctic ice, or conducting covert missions with Special Forces teams.

The transition from civilian life to military life under the authority of the U.S. Armed Forces takes place when a recruit signs the dotted line and reports for boot camp. The transformation of a civilian to a soldier takes a lot more than an agreement and just showing up someplace (sounds like church membership, doesn't it?).

The initial commitment and the act of "showing up" merely gets you in the door. Walking through the door merely marks the beginning of a process. Transformation is the fruit of transition.

Drastic changes must take place before any recruit is actually entrusted with a loaded weapon.[5] An even more dramatic transformation must take place to transform a raw recruit from the image of a civilian to the image of authority in any high-responsibility function. Long before any soldier is allowed to exercise authority, he or she must learn to live under authority.

The Roman centurion, a ranking Roman military officer mentioned in the gospels, illustrates the importance of living under authority before successfully assuming the image of authority.

**"Now when Jesus had entered Capernaum,
a centurion came to Him, pleading with Him, saying,**

'Lord, my servant is lying at home paralyzed, dreadfully tormented.' And Jesus said to him, 'I will come and heal him.'

The centurion answered and said, 'Lord, I am not worthy that You should come under my roof. But *only speak a word,* and my servant will be healed. *For I also am a man under authority,* having soldiers under me. And I say to this one, "Go," and he goes; and to another, "Come," and he comes; and to my servant, "Do this," and he does it.' When Jesus heard it, He marveled, and said to those who followed, 'Assuredly, I say to you, I have not found such great faith, not even in Israel!'" (Mt. 8:5-10, emphasis mine)

One Word Can Reshape Sad Reality

This Roman military leader recognized the image of authority in Jesus. He knew Jesus had absolute authority, and he knew instinctively that one word from Jesus would reshape the sad reality in his household.

"People and demons react in the face of the true image of authority. On the other hand, they mock every pretender they find. This is what happened to the seven sons of a prominent Jewish leader in Paul's day who pretended to have authority given in Jesus' name.

Then some of the itinerant Jewish exorcists took it upon themselves to call the name of the Lord Jesus over those who had evil spirits, saying, 'We exorcise you by the Jesus whom Paul preaches.' Also there were seven sons of Sceva, a Jewish chief priest, who did so. And the evil spirit answered and said, 'Jesus I know, and Paul I know; but *who are you?'*

Then the man in whom the evil spirit was leaped on them, overpowered them, and *prevailed against*

58 *them,* so that they fled out of that house naked and wounded. This became known both to all Jews and Greeks dwelling in Ephesus; and fear fell on them all, and *the name [the image] of the Lord Jesus was magnified.* And many who had believed came confessing and telling their deeds. Also, many of those who had practiced magic brought their books together and burned them in the sight of all. And they counted up the value of them, and it totaled fifty thousand pieces of silver. So the word of the Lord grew mightily and prevailed" (Acts 19:13-20).

They Were Just Sons of Adam Pretending...

These very religious sons of a prominent religious leader had rank, social position, and the appearance of power. The problem is that they were still sons of Adam who just pretended to know God.

It is easy to crucify these seven foolish men, but how many of us do *exactly* the same thing today? We pick up the name and image of Jesus just as we have heard others do—but without really knowing Him and walking in Him.

These men were publicly humiliated by the demonic powers in the man they prayed for because they were pretending to walk in a power they didn't possess.

The church—and many who attend church—walk through life totally powerless to change their own lives or to set others free. What is the problem? You must submit to the authority of Christ before you can walk in the authority of Christ. You can only operate from what is already inside you. You can go through life carrying a backpack full of Bibles and hauling a trailer full of Bibles behind your car...but it will do you no good until God's Word and His Spirit are inside your heart and ruling your life.

We know from the Scriptures that when you surrender to and cling to Christ, you become a life-giving spirit (again, see 1 Cor. 15:22, 45). If you are *not* a life-giving spirit, then you can't give life. When you pretend to be "in Christ" while actually living "in Adam," then you are just living (and lying).

You may be "saved, sanctified, and filled with the Holy Spirit." I urge you to ask yourself this question:

Am I content to go through the rest of my life carrying the pretend image others expect me to have, or am I willing to do what it takes to walk *in the image of Christ* and live as a bold witness to the fact that God is alive and well?

Your answer will determine whether you walk in the image of Adam or in the image of Christ from this day forward.

Endnotes

1. See Gen. 1:26.

2. W.E. Vine; F.F. Bruce, ed. (O.T.); *VINE'S Expository Dictionary of Old and New Testament Words* (Old Tappan, NJ: Fleming H. Revell Company, 1981), Greek #3686, onoma, on'-om-ah; from a presumed der. of the base of G1097 (comp. G3685); a "name" (lit. or fig.) [authority, character]:–called, (+ sur-) name (-d).*

3. Vine, *VINE'S Expository Dictionary of Old and New Testament Words,* N.T. Words, Volume 3: Lo–Ser, "name," (II) primary definition, p. 100.

4. *VINE'S, O.T. Words,* "image," p. 81.

5. The salvation experience is different from the military enlistment process in that the moment we repent and receive Christ, we are transformed from death to life. In that same moment, we gain a testimony that becomes a powerful weapon for leading others to Christ. So in this sense, the Lord gives each of us a "loaded weapon" upon conversion. In another sense, He Himself comes to dwell within us at that moment, making us "spiritual bombs walking."

Chapter 5
The First Adam Still Lives

Most of the people who call themselves Christians are homeless if you glance at the modern church in the West through the lens of spiritual discernment.

How can I say this? It is because most Christians *still* live and operate in the first Adam. Another way to put it is that many of us walk "in the flesh" and not in the Spirit.

In fact, Christians are "dead men walking" if they live in Adam. Why? When we walk in Adam while professing to walk in Christ, we essentially take up residence in a corpse awaiting burial. The term, "dead man walking" is a prison term used to describe the final walk of a man condemned to death on the day he walks from his cell to the execution chambers.

If we are in Christ, we are life-giving spirits *set free* from Adam's spiritual corpse in this life, and awaiting the resurrection and eternal reunification with God face to face.

If the old Adam nature is alive and well in our hearts, then the spirit man within us is struggling to survive or at least spiritually deaf and dumb, and Adam's image constantly pressures us to operate on the basis of our five senses.

The challenge facing most halfway saints is the unspoken conviction in their hearts and heads that says, "If I can't touch it, smell it, hear it, taste it, feel it or see it, then it isn't real."

That means that if you live "in Adam" then virtually everything you deal with is perceived and handled from your physical and mental abilities and resources—that includes your finances, your family, your close relationships, and even your "religious" activities.

"So what's so bad about that, Bishop?"

You cannot know God operating in the first Adam's state.

This is the problem: If you choose to walk and live solely in the natural realm, then you cut yourself off from the things of God! Paul warned the Christians in Corinth:

> "But the *natural man does not receive the things of the Spirit of God,* for they are foolishness to him; nor can he know them, because they are *spiritually discerned"* (1 Cor. 2:14, emphasis mine).

You cannot know God operating in the first Adam's state. You cannot even begin to understand the most basic fundamentals of the faith!

"But Bishop, I come to church every week!"

Showing up at the door isn't enough. It reminds me of every mother's nightmare, when her son bangs on the door wanting to show her something. She dries her hands and walks to the door only to find her offspring proudly holding up the carcass of some dead animal harvested from a nearby road, wooded area, or alley.

Even worse, the son holds up a snake he's managed to corner somewhere. Then he wonders why he can't waltz into the house like usual—it is because he is carrying something *dead* with him; he is walking with a serpent!

As I understand it, the Romans used to make an example of convicted murderers from time to time by permanently binding the corpse of their victim on their back. It was a grisly death sentence, since the putrid elements of decay eventually began to cross over to the living body of the host to ultimately destroy him.

Satan wants you to blindly strap on the rotting corpse of the old Adam in hopes that its decay will eventually quench the life of God in your own life. One thing is certain: Adam

still lives *outside* the house of God. Nothing of death or decay   **63**
will ever find its way into God's presence.

The Flesh (the First Adam) Lusts Against the Spirit

We have no business living in partnership with the "flesh"
or the first Adam. It can only bring grief and death. In the
words of the Apostle Paul: "I say then: Walk in the Spirit, and
you shall not fulfill the lust of the flesh. *For the flesh lusts
against the Spirit,* and the Spirit against the flesh; and these are
contrary to one another, so that you do not do the things that
you wish" (Gal. 5:16-17, emphasis mine).

The Apostle Paul lists a sample of 17 different products of
the "flesh" or the first Adam (including adultery, fornication,
uncleanness, lewdness, idolatry, sorcery, hatred, contentions,
jealousies, outbursts of wrath, selfish ambitions, dissensions,
heresies, envy, murders, drunkenness, and revelries).

Then Paul drops a bombshell on the compromising
church:

"... just as I also told you in time past, that *those
who practice such things will not inherit the kingdom of
God.* But the fruit of the Spirit is love, joy, peace, longsuffering, kindness, goodness, faithfulness, gentleness,
self- control. Against such there is no law" (Gal. 5:21-23,
emphasis mine).

We Try to Carry Our Favorite Sins into God's Kitchen

"Well, I don't understand, Bishop. I don't know what you're
talking about." Most of the time, people who say this kind of
thing are doing something they shouldn't, or are *not* doing
something they should. Too many of us want to waltz in and
out of God's "kitchen" carrying our favorite sins with us.

The Apostle Paul gets to the point in the Book of Galatians
when he says, "And those who are Christ's have crucified the

64 flesh with its passions and desires. If we live in the Spirit, let us also walk in the Spirit" (Gal 5:24-25).

To "walk in the Spirit" is the same as living "in Christ" and "walking with the last Adam." Most of us already know (on a personal level) what it means to walk in the flesh.

In a chapter entitled, "What Do You Believe" in my book, *What a Man Wants, What a Woman Needs,* I cited a quote that perfectly describes someone who is saved but still lives like the first Adam:

> **Oswald Chambers said, "We are taught to think like pagans and to live as Christians." In essence, we are taught to *think* in the flesh or to *think worldly* through life but somehow *live godly*. We can't have it both ways....[1]**

Most of us—if we are honest—feel very uncomfortable when we realize how closely we fit this description. We struggle day after day to justify our worldly thinking and carnal decision making while hoping to somehow live godly lives as well. It doesn't work and we know it.

Godly living has very little to do with our five senses because spiritual things must be spiritually discerned. The godly life has everything to do with the Spirit of the Lord, with God's Word, and with our ability to hear His voice and obey His will; so the natural senses only help a little.

Hypocrisy and double-mindedness carry a painful price tag. When adults adopt them as a lifestyle, they sometimes affect the future of an entire generation. One of the things I'm discovering about young people today is just how disconnected they are to the "modern" Christianity we are dishing out. They have a very low tolerance for hypocrisy (except in themselves).

Another Generation That Did Not Know the Lord   **65**

One of the verses in the Book of Judges just continues to haunt me. It says:

> **"When all that generation had been gathered to their fathers,** *another generation arose after them who did not know the LORD* **nor the work which He had done for Israel"** (Judges 2:10).

We have a whole generation coming up that doesn't even know God. They don't know the words to the Lord's prayer, how to finish a hymn, or what the Bible says about salvation, marriage, godly character, and eternal life. As soon as they get money, they spend it almost purely on impulse. Nothing is spiritually discerned; the natural man rules.

Do you wonder why there is so much killing, so much mugging, so much suicide, so much wild sex and unrestrained lifestyles today? It is because everything is based upon the information gathered by the five human senses and decided by the fallen first Adam nature.

If there is some "moral compass" or internal guidance system operating, it is purely secondary and submitted to the base emotions and desires of the first Adam nature. How did it happen? Why would an entire generation be "skipped" somehow?

Earlier generations perhaps demonstrated a greater value for morals than they did on money, but for whatever reason, it has flip-flopped today. This should be of great concern to the church. We must deliver this generation from themselves and from the first Adam.

We Refuse to Give Up Our "Dead Pets"

The problem is that the church is having a major "flip-flop problem" itself! Many in our current generation of Christians

DELIVER ME FROM ADAM

66 are actually first Adams who go to church faithfully but still live *outside* of God's house because they refuse to give up their "dead pets" (their entangling sins and the self-serving old Adam nature).

Since God cannot permit these things in His presence, we are faced with a clear choice. We must stop what we are doing, drop the dead and decaying things in our lives, and enter God's presence. It is our task in Christ to lead the next generation into a genuine knowledge of God.

The writer of Hebrews pinpointed at least part of the problem when he wrote:

> **"For though by this time *you* ought to be *teachers*, you need someone to teach you again the first principles of the oracles of God; and *you have come to need milk and not* solid food. For everyone who partakes only of milk is unskilled in the word of righteousness, *for he is a babe.* But solid food belongs to those who are of full age, that is, those who by reason of use have their senses exercised *to discern both good and evil*"** (Heb. 5:12-14, emphasis mine).

Too Busy Changing our Nursing Stations

If you've been saved more than three years, then you ought to be a teacher in the sense that you are taking younger Believers in tow and making disciples of them in the things of the Lord. Yet too many of us are too busy "changing our nursing stations" based on the pastor's perceived ability to feed us what we want.

That is what concerns me about "church-jumpin' folk." They will complain to anyone who will listen, "Well, I left that church because they don't do enough teaching." My question is, "What about your responsibility to teach yourself?"

We go to a church service for maybe 90 minutes a week and then check out and go home. (Some folks spend more

time in a tanning booth, a nail salon, or the local health spa).   **67**
So they go through the whole week and then complain that
they haven't been taught—it is because you won't teach yourself. You refuse to study to show yourself approved unto God
(see 2 Tim. 2:15). Don't put the burden of the teaching on
your preacher. You have a personal responsibility to learn and
know God's Word.

The Apostle Paul was concerned about older believers who
were still infants in their faith, and so should we! He said,
"You have come to need milk and not solid food." What does
that mean?

I Don't Want to Hear That— I Need a Hand Out

It means, in other words: "I don't want deep stuff, preacher.
Don't give me any of that Kingdom stuff, just stay with that
grace and mercy stuff. That's what I need. Give me some
of that 'I'm pitiful' stuff, give me that 'I can fall down and
God will always pick me up' stuff. But don't make me feel
responsible, and don't tell me this is the age of possibility. I'm
not interested when you say I can stand up and move in this
hard season. Above all, don't tell me I can rule in the midst of
mine enemies. I don't want to hear that—I need a hand out."

Sometimes, the impact and "insult value" of hard-hitting
scripture passages suffer in the translation from language to
language. That seems to be the case where Paul says, "For
though by this time you ought to be teachers, you need someone to teach you again… you have come to need milk and not
solid food. For everyone who partakes only of milk…is a
babe" (Heb. 5:12-13).

Next time you go to church, look at your neighbors and
imagine them in a crib with Pampers. God is telling us
through the Apostle Paul, "That chair next to you is a crib and
the person in it is wearing a baby's diaper! Whenever they
make a mess (and they certainly will), they want you (or the
preacher) to change them."

(To be honest, it is very hard for me to shake hands at the end of a service at times because so many spiritually delayed babies come up to me wanting me to change their diapers.)

When Paul said, "But solid food belongs to those who are of full age, that is, those who by reason of use have their senses exercised to discern both good and evil (Heb. 5:14, emphasis mine); he was saying that if you cannot come out of Adam, then you will never be able to discern between good and evil.

Why Do I Fall Again and Again?

Many Christians wonder why they constantly fall into the same old sins and temptations again and again. The answer is right in front of us—we must shed the old Adam with all of his ways and walk in Christ.

Those who walk into our churches—from any generation —carrying the first Adam on their backs should be able to walk out in Christ, the last Adam. Nothing less will do. The only way any of us can judge between good and evil is to walk holy in Christ so our spirits can accurately discern what God is saying.

In the first Adam state, we are constantly seeking the approval of someone else. It becomes a driving compulsion that dominates our lives. Once again, we must return to the very beginning to see how this compulsion got there and why it takes God's intervention to remove it.

We have to be delivered from the state of Adam. According to the Bible, this is how it all began.

"So when the woman *saw* that the tree was good for food, that it was pleasant to the eyes, and a tree desirable to make one wise, she took of its fruit and ate. She also gave to her husband with her, and he ate" (Gen. 3:6, emphasis mine).

What did the first woman do? She saw; she did not **69** spiritually discern (this isn't a "woman" problem, men do exactly the same thing). This is the process of the fall and of the fallen nature of Adam—and it is still the nature of the first Adam right now. This was the process: **She saw. He saw. They fell.**

They fell. There wasn't anything spiritual about what they did. This is our challenge and primary pitfall as human beings: Most of us see, and because we see, we have desire.

God created Adam in perfection first. He gave Adam the breath of life, blessed him, put him in the Garden, gave him total dominion, and allowed him to name the animals. Then God gave him an extra surprise when He fashioned a woman from his rib and gave Eve to him as a helpmate. Adam must have said at that point, "Woo, this is something here!"

But at the same time, at the moment of truth, Adam was suddenly faced with a choice he had never imagined before: please God or please Eve?

Do you realize that most of us face similar choices throughout our lives? People we love, people we like, and even people we secretly despise, will present things to us that seem to go against the fundamental teachings of God and our understanding of right and wrong. Most of us will be seriously tempted to go along with them too. Why? It is because we really want everyone to like us. No one enjoys being rejected or disliked.

Living for the Anticipated Response of Others

Although I would like to think I'm "above" all of that, I know I am not. Virtually everything I do is done with the opinions of others in mind in some way or another. The anticipated responses of other people seem to affect most of our thinking and behavior.

(Some of this serves a good purpose. God uses godly peer

DELIVER ME FROM ADAM

70 pressure to help us live godly lives, but it is barely noticeable compared to the power of Jesus Christ at work in us.)

The first Adam, however, is ruled and dominated by the compulsion to please others (or to please self). When you get dressed for work, for a meeting, or for a church service, you spend time preparing your hair, choosing your clothing, and checking your appearance in the mirror.

Whether you spend a little time or a lot, when you look in the mirror, it isn't just to see if you look good to yourself. No, you are looking with the thought in your mind, "What will other people think or say?" (Yes, you do it even if you are a man.)

One reason I know I am not exempt from this process comes from my experiences early in my college years. I used to have a friend there whom I will call "Kevin". We grew up together, so we had a long history.

No matter how well I dressed, Kevin could always find what was out of order. He would walk into the party or social event, look at me, and say, "Eddie, that suit looks good, but you need to shine your shoes."

It didn't matter that I left home feeling good about myself and my appearance that night, because once Kevin picked out my shoes, then everything else was null and void. I couldn't wait until I could get back home because I spent the rest of the evening hiding my feet and feeling bad. Why? Because I was seeking approval and one person's negative statement messed up my day.

How Many Days Were Messed Up by Other People?

Ask yourself: "How many days of my life have been messed up by someone who said something carelessly?" In almost every case, your critic probably went on with the day without a thought while you remained focused on their negative comment: "Eddie, don't you know your tie doesn't quite match your shirt?"

Listen, if something looks good to you, then it doesn't **71** matter what Kevin, Mary, Harry, or Jammel has to say about it. If some negative joker tries to say your tie doesn't match your clothes, or that your shoes don't match your blouse, then look them in the eye and say, "Babe, you don't know the new fashion, do you? This is the new fashion. I am a forerunner. I'm sorry, but you are the one living behind the times. Nobody wears match-ups anymore." Make up your mind in Christ: I am not going to let a mere man or woman intimidate me!

We've already learned that you cannot know God operating in the first Adam's state, and that we are constantly faced with a choice that pits God's kingdom of the spirit against all of the attractions and temptations of the fallen world—including the approval and acceptance of other people.

One of the principles that helps us keep our goal in sight is the law of sowing and reaping. The Bible says, "Do not be deceived, God is not mocked; for whatever a man sows, that he will also reap. For he who sows to his flesh will of the flesh reap corruption, but he who sows to the Spirit will of the Spirit reap everlasting life" (Gal 6:7-8, emphasis mine). This helps explain why Adam still lives outside of God's house.

Fence-straddlers Never Win

Is there another reason we need to be delivered from Adam? Yes. It has to happen if we ever hope to move into what God has ordained for us. Fence-straddlers never win races (except in politics), and they rarely arrive at any destination worth having.

The Apostle James said: "A double minded man is unstable in all his ways" (Jas. 1:8, KJV). Too many Christians try to cling to their dead Adam while stepping across the line into God's presence. It doesn't work.

Worldly thinking and godly living are totally incompatible. They are mutually exclusive terms—in

other words, they don't get along, and they don't mix without disastrous results.

The dangers of the double-minded life became a major focus of the apostle John later in his life. Perhaps he knew the true meaning of the Greek word, *dipsuchos,* translated as "double-minded" in English. It means "two-spirited, i.e., vacillating (in opinion or purpose)....

"Two-spirited" people try to straddle the dividing line between darkness and light, the invisible boundary between the created world *(kosmos)* and the eternal kingdom of God. This impossible spiritual gymnastic feat produces only instability.[2]

Adam and Eve Were Afraid They Might Miss Something

A life lived in the first Adam is all based on fear. Adam and Eve fell for the serpent's bait because they were afraid they might be missing something that God was withholding from them. The serpent hooked them with a fear-laced statement:

"Then the serpent said to the woman, 'You will not surely die. *For God knows* that in the day you eat of it your eyes will be opened, and you will be like God, knowing good and evil'" (Gen. 3:4-5, emphasis mine).

How much life has been sucked out of you by fear about "something that might or might not happen?" Even as you read these words, you may be struggling to focus on their meaning because you are thinking about something that might happen to you.

Most of the time the things we fear don't come to pass. Even if they do, we have wasted a day and given the fear more power than it deserved. We allowed the fear of the future to torture us long before the thing happened.

God gives each of us a whole good day of life, but we tend to mess it up with fear while ignoring the answer Jesus shared with us in one simple prayer:

> **"Our Father in heaven, Hallowed be Your name. Your kingdom come. Your will be done on earth as it is in heaven. *Give us this day our daily bread.* And forgive us our debts, as we forgive our debtors. And do not lead us into temptation, but deliver us from the evil one. For Yours is the kingdom and the power and the glory forever. Amen"** (Mt. 6:9-13, emphasis mine).

This prayer begins with a phrase reserved for family: *Our Father.* You speak it from *inside* the Father's household, not from outside His presence where dead things stay. If you pray the prayer and believe it, then God blesses your bread for the day.

Yes, you might have some things come up that you will have to deal with tomorrow, but you might as well eat the bread your Father gave you for today. When tomorrow comes, then pray the same prayer and walk in His provision. The following day, pray the same prayer and trust your Heavenly Father for what you need that day.

If you sit up worrying about tomorrow, then you won't eat the bread you have today. When tomorrow comes, you may end up being too weak to fight through it anyway because you never got the joy you needed at the moment that God gave it to you.

Most of us fail to live fully in the moment because we are afraid of what may happen tomorrow, and we insist on clinging to Adam's dead ways. That deprives us of Christ's abundant life now, and contaminates the future with fear and anxiety. God has a much better way: He calls us to *walk in the Spirit and live in Christ.*

1. Eddie L. Long, *What a Man Wants, What a Woman Needs* (Nashville, TN: Thomas Nelson Publishers, a division of Thomas Nelson, Inc., 2002), 37.

2. Ibid, p. 38.

I'm Your Friend:
Don't Manipulate Me

Manipulation was the first characteristic Eve displayed after she ate the forbidden fruit in the Garden of Eden. We know this because her first act after receiving "the knowledge of good and evil" was to manipulate her gullible husband into eating the fruit with her. The Bible says "She took of its fruit and ate. She also gave to her husband with her, and he ate" (Gen. 3:6b).

We know that they received the knowledge of good and evil because when they heard God approaching them, they realized He was *good* and they were *evil*. Adam makes the first mention of fear in the Bible when he finally answers God's call: "I heard Your voice in the garden, and *I was afraid* because I was naked; and I hid myself" (Gen. 3:10b, emphasis mine).

When God asked Adam if he had eaten from the tree, the man first blamed God for giving him Eve in the first place; then he blamed Eve for offering him the fruit (see Gen. 3:11-12). The blame game didn't work then, and it doesn't work now. Yet we still fall for the temptation to manipulate God with our excuses, finger pointing, and juggling of justifications.

Thanks to fear, manipulation remains one of humanity's favorite survival tools. Most of us keep looking to the future as a door of escape from today's failures and disappointments, or even worse, fearing the unknown "something" that might happen. When we live in Adam's state, we try to control our fear and win the approval of people and of God Himself by manipulating and controlling every variable we can in our environment.

We Control and Manipulate for Our Own Advantage

Most of us would hate to admit it, but we sometimes feel a need to control and manipulate for our own comfort and advantage. We may camouflage our control techniques under spiritually correct terms such as "maintaining order" or "helping to organize and direct others"; but we are still known by our "fruits" or actions (see Luke, 6:44).

The biggest crack in the foundation of our lives is our misunderstanding of what love really is and how it functions in real life. This is a serious problem because love relates directly to our true image in Christ, and it is absent or distorted in Adam's image.

God gave us *His* definition of love in Paul's letter to the Corinthians, and this is the way you and I will live once we are delivered from Adam's image and begin confidently walking in Christ's image:

> "Though I speak with the tongues of men and of angels, but have not love, I have become sounding brass or a clanging cymbal. And though I have the gift of prophecy, and understand all mysteries and all knowledge, and though I have all faith, so that I could remove mountains, but have not love, I am nothing. And though I bestow all my goods to feed the poor, and though I give my body to be burned, but have not love, it profits me nothing. Love suffers long and is kind; love does not envy; love does not parade itself, is not puffed up; does not behave rudely, does not seek its own, is not provoked, thinks no evil; does not rejoice in iniquity, but rejoices in the truth; bears all things, believes all things, hopes all things, endures all things. Love never fails" (1 Cor. 13:1-8a).

Jesus Christ personally *demonstrated* it on the cross when **77** He laid down His life for us. He is the one who said:

> "**This is My commandment, that you love one another as I have loved you.** *Greater love has no one than this, than to lay down one's life for his friends.* **You are My friends if you do whatever I command you**" (John 15:12-14, emphasis mine).

We've all heard and seen the news stories about the different ways people act in crisis. When the "unsinkable" ocean cruiser called the *Titanic* began to sink, desperate men sometimes pushed women and children aside to save themselves (while others gave up their lives to save strangers).

When New York's World Trade Center Towers were attacked by terrorists, hundreds of selfless men and women rushed back into the upper floors and smoke-filled stairwells hoping to save lives—only to lose their own.

It is sad that the biggest problem the modern church faces is its own sorry reputation for being cruel and unloving to its own and to outsiders. Wherever you go, it seems you will find people who are angry about hypocrisy in church folk—and most of them *are* church folk who have "been done wrong" by other church folk.

Love Does Not Try to Control

The problem is that we don't understand love. *Love never attempts to control others.* Love does not seek it's own—it doesn't demand its own way. Love gives unconditionally.

Often we surround ourselves with a group of people that we feel we can manipulate, control, or at least enjoy their favor most of the time. We turn on the manipulation or controlling influence whenever we need to be pumped-up emotionally, or whenever we need a posse of positive supporters.

In virtually every area of our lives, we catch ourselves trying to control situations, to "tell our side" of the story, or trying to impose our personal desires on someone else.

We know we've crossed the line when our inner circle of family and friends chooses not to cooperate with our desires. Sometimes we may react emotionally by telling them they don't care about us.

Being a friend does not mean that a person has to submit to being controlled by you or anyone else. I may be your friend, but that doesn't mean that I have to like everything you like or do whatever you say do.

Don't Try to Manipulate Me--Love Me Anyway

The truth is that I might not like everything you like. That does not mean I am not your friend. Don't try to manipulate me. Don't try to control me. Don't try to hold me down. Love me anyway, in spite of our differences. Love is unconditional.

If the Lord had no problem using the marriage relationship to illustrate His relationship with the Church, then we are free to learn from marriage in the area of relationships within the church.

You have nothing but problems in a marriage when the partners involved are essentially two manipulating people with a lust for self-pleasure and needy egos. They tend to look to each other all the time to be pumped up, pleased, pleasured, and put in first place. They constantly try to manipulate each other into satisfying their own desires instead of just serving and loving one another.

To take things to another level, you have nothing but problems in a local church body when the leaders involved are essentially manipulating people with a lust for self-pleasure and needy egos. They tend to look to the congregation, the service structure, and formulas all the time to be pumped up, pleased, pleasured, and put in first place.

They constantly try to manipulate God, each other, and the congregation into satisfying their own personal desires and egotistical needs instead of serving and loving one another in Christ.

To manipulate is "to control or play upon by artful, unfair, or insidious means, especially to one's advantage; and to change by artful or unfair means so as to serve one's purpose."[1]

Manipulation is deadly to relationships at every level. This illegal pressure to force our way or desires on others create incredible problems in the lives of others. I sometimes wonder if it is manipulation and control that helps keep church counselors, psychologists and psychiatrists working year after year!

Manipulating and Being Manipulated

The Bible speaks of people who go about "deceiving and being deceived" (2 Tim. 3:13b). I'm convinced a whole lot of us go around "manipulating and being manipulated." The root of it all seems to be fear, especially the fear of rejection, abandonment and failure.

Even well-meaning parents fall into tricks of manipulation with children in moments of frustration or fatigue. They may say, "Mommy won't love you unless you do what I say" or "If you want Daddy to spend time with you then you'll have to make me proud of you."

This kind of subtle manipulation may set up a "salvation by works" or "earn my love" mindset that can be deadly. Parental love, the love among friends, marital love, and Christian love are *unconditional.* We love in spite of failure, disappointment, weakness, or frustration.

How can we kill the spirit of manipulation in the church? The Bible says:

"For God has not given us *a spirit of fear,* but of power and of love and of a sound mind. Therefore *do*

not be ashamed of the testimony of our Lord, nor of me His prisoner, but share with me in the sufferings for the gospel according to the power of God, who has saved us and called us with a holy calling, not according to our works, but according to His own purpose and grace which was given to us in Christ Jesus before time began.... For this reason I also suffer these things; nevertheless I am not ashamed, for I know whom I have believed and am persuaded that He is able to keep what I have committed to Him until that Day" (2 Tim 1:7-9, 12; emphasis mine).

What is this urge, this compulsion to control and struggle for approval? What drives you to fight and squabble for external power in your life? It is your ego.

Remember what we learned previously: *Your ego is not who you really are.* Your ego is an artificial image that you create within yourself based primarily on the opinions and approval of others around you. In essence, it is your social mass.

Adam Discarded the Divine Image and Made His Own

The first Adam brought about a self-image. When he took the fruit, he discarded the divine image God gave him and began to create his own image and likeness modeled after his new mentor—the serpent. This immediately produced pain.

Don't expect anyone to pray you out of ego pain. You have to personally decide to step out of it. God has already provided the cure, given the solution, and made things new. The next step starts with you.

Our Transformation Begins With a Personal Decision

If I have created a "bishop problem," an ego thing that constantly seeks approval and favor through a title, then it is up to me to recognize it for what it is and stop my efforts to control and manipulate with a name. No matter who or "what" we are, our transformation from Adam's image to the image of Christ begins with a personal decision.

With God's help, I discovered that I had spent fifty years letting other people "mess with Buddy"—my ego. I was thinking all along that "Buddy" was me, but my ego is not me. The title "bishop" isn't me either.

I'm a man created by God to serve, not to be served (see the Lord's example in Mt. 20:28). If Jesus washed the disciples's feet, that is what you and I need to be doing. This is the practical side of "having the mind of Christ" (see 1 Cor. 2:16b).

Once I recognize my problem and leave Adam's image at the foot of the cross, then I will stop manipulating my friends, my family members, and my church family. The last Adam deals with people totally different than the first Adam.

> **"Therefore if there is any consolation in Christ, if any comfort of love, if any fellowship of the Spirit, if any affection and mercy, fulfill my joy by being like-minded, having the same love, being of one accord, of one mind.** *Let nothing be done through selfish ambition or conceit,* **but in lowliness of mind** *let each one esteem others better than himself.* **Let each of you look out not only for his own interests, but also for the interests of others"** (Phil. 2:1-4, emphasis mine).

Did you hear what God said in these verses? Now this is a hard pill to swallow. God doesn't address people in the flesh; He speaks to people who are in Christ. He is saying that *humility comes when you live in the last Adam.*

God doesn't exclude people from His love based on how they dress, how they talk, how they act, or even on how they smell! He said that if there is "any consolation in Christ," then you and I will *not* judge others or consider ourselves to be better than anyone else.[2]

82 Then the Lord summarizes things through the Apostle Paul: "Let each of you look out not only for his own interests..." (see Phil. 2:4, emphasis mine).

Messing Up our Sunday Religion

These scriptures really mess up our Sunday religion and comfortable pew-based Christianity. They clash with the attitudes most of us wear when we come to church.

"I need my word. I've come for my breakthrough. Yes sir, I need *my* blessing' for the week. Now what is that hussy doin' in my place? I've been sittin' there for 25 years, and I've worn the cushions down to fit just right!"

People in general like to judge others, but it seems we get a second wind when we get saved because we think we have a right to judge everyone we meet!

"Oh, their hair just isn't right."

"No, they aren't any good." "Well, did you hear the way she was talking?"

I Ought to Have My Own TV Court Program

It seems that church people are some of the most judgmental people on the planet. Judgmental attitudes seem to suck energy from the soul, but some of us are so busy judging people that we think we ought to have our own TV court program. That way we could parade all of our brothers and sisters before the bench and publicly pronounce our judgments on them.

We have one big problem blocking our hopes as amateur self-proclaimed judges: God's Word. Jesus said:

"Therefore be merciful, just as your Father also is merciful. *Judge not, and you shall not be judged.*

Condemn not, and you shall not be condemned. **Forgive,**
and you will be forgiven" (Luke 6:36-37, emphasis
mine).

Judging by the way most of us judge others, we are in for
a rough time in God's courtroom. I don't want to hear God's
sentence of condemnation for people who have made a career
out of condemning others.

Jesus was very clear. If you don't want to be judged, then
don't judge others. If you don't want to be condemned, then
don't condemn others. If you want mercy, then show mercy.
If you want forgiveness, you have to forgive.

Stop Judging People and Live

If you ignore God's Word and constantly judge others, it
will begin to weigh on you. Before long, it will begin to suck
the life out of you. *Stop judging people and live.* Stop being so
offended and live.

Too many of us remain trapped in the past by wounded
egos. We are still stuck at the place and time we (the false
"Adam image" of ourselves) were hurt by something that
happened long ago.

Deal with today. You are who you are because of the spirit
of God within you, not because of the outward things that
happened to you. You are still God's child—you could be
dead, but you are still alive and invested with God-given destiny and purpose.

Why focus on things from the past that you can't change?
Instead, you can celebrate what God has given you today? You
may find yourself in a situation like mine, where I allowed the
"Buddy" that I created—the false self-image that has nothing
to do with the image of God—to wrestle with the real me in
Christ and mess with my destiny in God's Kingdom.

Shake Off the Dust and Don't Get an Attitude

We tend to spend a lot of time and energy avoiding rejection, and it isn't hard to understand why. Rejection hurts. But Jesus told the disciples, "When ya'll go to these houses, if they don't receive you then just shake off the dust from your shoes. Don't get an attitude" ("Eddie's version" of Mark 6:11).

If somebody walked out on you in a marriage or partnership, leaving you feeling totally destroyed, then perhaps God wants to show you something. You are special, and you really don't need those shaky people props. He has you covered, supported, upheld, and defended on every side.

Remember: That person can only walk out once; unless you keep creating the situation over and over again. When you do that, you give them power over your life and destiny that they don't need, deserve, and value.

God never walks out. He is always in, He will never leave you nor forsake you, and He will literally work wonders! He will guard, guide, and prosper you as long as you can serve Him and humble yourself.

On the other hand, the image of the first Adam quickly forgets the warnings of God. I'm thinking of the passage that says, "God resists the proud, but gives grace to the humble" (James 4:6). Pride and overbearing ways are popular tools of manipulation and control in the world of Adam, but they are worthless to people in Christ.

It is time for us to get our heads out the sky and drop our grand ways. Every pattern of hypocrisy has to go—we must stop looking over the shoulders of the people we're talking to in hopes of finding someone more interesting, useful, or valuable to our social status.

Unwrapped and Undecorated Packages

God knows you intimately. He knows every battle you face and every temptation you entertain each day. It is just like

Him to send your blessing or answer to prayer in an "unwrapped and undecorated package" that doesn't fit your preconceived ideas.

God said the things of the Spirit can only be perceived and received in the Spirit. The flesh—the first Adam image—is blind to the things of the Spirit.

I've warned the people in my congregation at New Birth Missionary Baptist Church, "Don't you break your neck trying to speak to me and pass ten people in the process without saying a word. Your blessing is probably being carried by one of the ten saints you bypassed, not by me. *God can use anybody.*"

When you enter a meeting or step outside of your door each morning, God has already "ordered your steps" if you trust and obey Him. The Bible says, "The steps of a good man are ordered by the Lord, and He delights in his way" (Ps. 37:23).

That means you are on divine assignment today, and you will be on assignment tomorrow. He already knows where you were going to sit and who will sit by you at lunch, on the bus, or at the business seminar. Not only will He supply what you need each day, but He will also put something in you that someone else desperately needs to receive.

If you are struggling with the dangerous habit of manipulating and controlling others, then God may have to administer an overdose of humility to help you realize that apart from Him you wouldn't be anything or have anything. Stop being so arrogant. Once you fully receive the image of Christ, then He expects you to humbly give and share what you have received. It was Jesus who sent His disciples out with the words:

> "And as you go, preach, saying, 'The kingdom of heaven is at hand.' Heal the sick, cleanse the lepers, raise the dead, cast out demons. *Freely you have received, freely give*" (Mt. 10:7-8, emphasis mine).

If you have received anything at all from God, then you

need to give it and bless someone. If you see someone walking, then ask the Lord if He wants you to give that person a ride.

God's Blessings are Never Just For You

Don't testify about the car, the clothes, and the income God gave you if you are unwilling to use them for the Kingdom. The blessings of God are never given merely for your benefit alone. Remember the days when you had to walk to work or wear hand-me-down clothes. What you do for others today in the image of Christ, lays the groundwork for what you *will* have tomorrow.

Even if we have read the Bible from cover to cover countless times, we still tend to forget the secret of Job. He got his breakthrough only after he prayed for his doubt-filled, unbelieving friends. When Job prayed for his friends, God released him from his affliction and blessed him with double for everything he lost.

The key to your breakthrough is in your ability to pray for someone else's breakthrough.

I just want others to get blessed, because I've learned some things about the financial principles of the Kingdom of God. If I invest faith and prayer for others to get blessed, then I won't doubt that God Almighty is still working. I am assured He will finally get around to me in His good time.

"Let each of you look out not only for his own interests, but also for the interests of others" (Phil. 2:4).

All of this sounds simple, but you and I both struggle on an internal battleground called the mind. Once we break the manipulation habit, we face another battle for control of our thoughts and memories. In essence, we are all "stuck in time with a bad movie."

1. *Merriam Webster's Collegiate Dictionary, Tenth Edition,* p. 708, from the second primary definition for "manipulate."

2. For the record, this statement is not a veiled support for "universalism" in which everyone is saved and no one goes to hell. Nor is it meant to imply that the Lord does not care whether or not we live unholy lives filled with profanity, immorality, or uncleanliness. It specifically concerns the way blood-washed Christians treat other blood-washed Christians; and the way we represent Jesus Christ to those who are not yet saved.

Chapter 7
Stuck In Time With a Bad Movie

Hollywood released a movie several years ago about a self-centered weathercaster who was trapped in time in a small Pennsylvania town. He was doomed to relive Groundhog's Day over and over until he changed his character.

Fiction often imitates fact.

God gave us vivid memories so we could remember lessons learned, treasure memories of loved ones, and remember His faithfulness from generation to generation.

When you live in the image of the first Adam and think your mind is really "you," then your memory seems doomed to "turn against you." It creates huge problems when your mind forces you back in time again and again by rerunning memory clips—whether you want to remember the scenes or not.

How many times have you heard people say something like: "God just didn't want me to have fun! Why did He make me wait to have sex until after I was married? It just doesn't make sense."

God isn't limited to doing things that fit into our puny minds—and He always knows what He is talking about. Since He created you, He knows that if you have sexual experiences before you get married, then you will have memory clips or mental flashbacks of "Person A" even in intimate moments with your spouse.

What happens to your thought life and emotions in that moment if your mind tells you that your partner "isn't doing things like the person in the memory clip that was so enjoyable?"

It is true that your mind is not you, but you will still

90 experience some problems and complications if you have a memory clip or flashback in your mind saying, "This is the way I want it...."

"Oh, That's Just a 'Memory Clip' of Another Lover"

What if your spouse decides to ask the unspoken question, "How do you *know* how you want it?" You may be able to divert the conversation and avoid saying, "Oh, that is because I have a 'memory clip' of another lover playing through my mind."

Given the tendency of the mouth to speak out what is in the heart and mind, it is virtually inevitable that your mouth will betray your thoughts. One night you will call him Leroy when his name is John (or you will say Mary when her name is Maureen).

The Apostle Paul talked about our wrestling match with sin using himself as an example:

> "For we know that the law is spiritual, but I am carnal, sold under sin. For what I am doing, I do not understand. For what I will to do, that I do not practice; but *what I hate, that I do*.... For the good that I will to do, I do not do; but the evil I will not to do, that I practice" (Rom. 7:14-15, 19; emphasis mine).

Paul was basically saying, "I don't do the good stuff that I want to do, and I keep doing the bad stuff I don't want to do! Why? Because I've allowed my mind—the first Adam kind of mind—to have control over me. My mind keeps running back memory clips of my sins and mistakes...."

Stuck in Our Memories

Too many of us are reliving things that are stuck in our memories. Remember this fact: You are not your experience.

"But Bishop, what about the stuff that happened to me when I was a kid...I was molested, I was rejected..."

You are not what you experienced – unless you allow your mind to keep refreshing the memories, trauma, and emotions of those painful or sinful experiences. That is how you allow your mind to "become you."

"Bishop, this may shock you but I am no longer a woman."
"Why?"
"'Cause my daddy did this..."
"No, you are still a woman, created in the image of God. You still have your femininity. What you suffered and experienced *is not you.*"

When you carry too much pain from the past, you will nearly always say things like, "A few years from now...when things get better, I'll do this." What are you going to do now? If you spend all of your time in the past or in the future, you're never here.

Perhaps you can't get your marriage on track because you still remember how your spouse was when you were first married. If you think you are your mind, then you aren't operating in the image of God.

Doomed to Relive the Past

You will keep remembering what happened back then and holding it against your spouse as if you are doomed to relive the past even into your future. Your obsession with the past keeps you from stepping into "today" to forgive.

Jesus taught that prayer should include the vital component of forgiveness. "Forgive us our debts, as we forgive our debtors..." (Mt. 6:12). That means, "God, forgive me as I forgive others." Now if you can't forgive, you are telling God to

forgive you only up to the point where you can forgive others.
The image of Christ forgives!

"Why can't you forgive them?"
"Aw, you don't know what they've done…"

No, but it is clear what *you* have done. You just authorized your mind—your life laptop—to remind you of what they did in living full-motion color.
When?
Yesterday.
Which causes you to do what?
Miss life right now.
Where is the Spirit of the Lord?
Here and now.
How does He minister to me?
In the *here and now.*
What am I supposed to do?
Get into His presence.
When?
Now!
"But Bishop, if you tell me to operate outside of my five senses, then it forces me to get into the Spirit."
Yes, that's what I'm saying.

The Mind and Physical Senses May Imprison Us in Time

Your mind, working in concert with your five physical senses, tries to hold you or imprison you in time. You keep remembering "a time," and it keeps you from walking in the Spirit because the Spirit transcends time.

God wants to lift you out of time and pull you out of your pain. He wants to break you out of your perpetual anticipation (of future events) and your unending memory bank (of past events). Why? He wants you to focus on what He is doing now. This is where you enjoy all of His blessings, forgiveness, **93** grace, mercy, and healing.

If you aren't *here* and *now,* then we could pray all day for you and you still wouldn't get healed. In what time frame did Jesus pray? He said, "Give us *this day* our daily bread" (Mt. 6:11).

I wonder if our Heavenly Father echoes the question so many pastors want to ask their complaining, hooky-playing members:

"How can I give you your daily bread when you won't show up (in church) to pick up your loaf?"

"Well you don't understand. I was hurt by a pastor. In fact, I was hurt by you—you didn't return my call."

So you're sitting there right now but you aren't hearing me because you keep watching the memory clip playing over and over in your mind, 'He didn't call me when I needed him.'

Once your mind is no longer a tool—it has become your enemy.

God is always there, even when your pastor or friend cannot come to your aid. No matter how much men and women may want to come to your aid, they may be faced with another crisis or conflict that is even worse than your own!

This is the problem: Once your mind is no longer a tool—it has become your enemy.

The Bible says, "For as [a man] thinks in his heart, so is he" (Prov. 23:7), but it is not saying your mind is "you." The writer of Proverbs is speaking of the heart, not the head. This is where our image resides—either the fallen and self-centered image of Adam or the image of God.

"Will you set your eyes on that which is not? For riches certainly make themselves wings; they fly away like

94   an eagle toward heaven. Do not eat the bread of a miser, nor desire his delicacies; for as he thinks *in his heart,* so is he. 'Eat and drink!' he says to you, but *his heart* is not with you" (Prov. 23:5-7, emphasis mine).

There is a big difference between letting your mind work for you as your servant and letting it run things. Bondage (to the past and future) comes when you believe and live as if your mind is the real you.

Focus on the Same Things Christ Did

The *truth* is that you were created and transformed through Jesus Christ to walk in the image of Christ. Just focus on the same things Christ did.

The Bible calls Jesus the "author" or pioneer of our faith: "Looking unto *Jesus, the author and finisher of our faith,* who for the joy that was set before Him endured the cross, despising the shame, and has sat down at the right hand of the throne of God" (Heb. 12:2, emphasis mine). He is the trailblazer of God-pleasing living.

For one thing, Paul said that Jesus Christ really didn't focus on making a grand reputation for Himself:

"Let this mind be in you which was also in Christ Jesus, who, being in the form of God, did not consider it robbery to be equal with God, but *made Himself of no reputation,* taking the form of a bondservant, and coming in the likeness of men. And being found in appearance as a man, *He humbled Himself* and became obedient to the point of death, even the death of the cross" (Phil. 2:5-8, emphasis mine).

Jesus Chose Humility, We Choose Career Portfolios

Jesus humbled Himself, but what do we do? Most of us

seem to focus on writing power resumes and producing effective career portfolios for maximum impact.

Do you know what I do when I get a resume? I discount everything claimed by 50 percent because I know that at least half of it is probably a lie! It is nothing but marketing—the image of Adam motivates most of us to make ourselves into something other than what we are.

If you want to know the truth about it, you will be known in heaven by your servanthood, not by your rulership. What did the Bible say about Jesus? "For even the Son of Man did not come to be served, but to serve [as a servant], and to give His life a ransom for many" (Mark 10:45, emphasis and insertion mine).

Jesus went even further than that when He told His disciples, "If anyone desires to be first, he shall be last of all and servant of all" (Mark 9:35b, emphasis mine).

To the degree that you will be a servant, that is the degree to which you can rule. So the first thing to settle is not that you can "run" something, but that you can serve someone. If you can serve others in the image and footsteps of Christ Jesus, God will elevate you.

Unfortunately, we don't do things that way. We believe what our minds tell us more than we believe the Word of God. If other people say we just have to create our own self-promotion campaign, then we believe it. The idea that we should humble ourselves just doesn't seem to make any sense in today's cut-throat world. We rely on our bragging power. "You must not know who I am!" No, you must not know who you are.

We Put All Our Trust in Our Own Program

Most of us live in perpetual fear (but we hate to admit it) because our minds have convinced us to put all of our trust in our own program—even though we know just how flawed our program really is. We don't know what God ordained and assigned to us.

This is the root problem: We live in fear because we are trying to protect this image that isn't us. We are doomed to live in fear as long as we refuse to spend time with God so He can show us who we are and reveal our divine assignment.

You will never begin to live until you know how you are supposed to end. *Once you know how you are supposed to end, then all the powers in hell can't stop you!*

Once you discover your true image in Christ and break out of the time lock with a bad movie from your past—your whole way of thinking changes.

If you land in a hard situation, your last Adam image might think:

> *"Oh...my computer—my mind—is telling me the truth right now. It is reminding me of God's Word instead of past failures and fears. I'm not finished, and that means you can't take me out. I'm not leaving, so sickness can't take me out! God still has some things for me to do. I'm not depressed because I know my enemies and these obstacles can't take me out. I have some things to finish, and I'm not even halfway through!"*

Jesus Refused a "Reputation"

Jesus made Himself "of no reputation" (Phil. 2:8). That means He actively avoided things that would produce a "reputation" among His flesh-centered peers. When He worked miracles, He often told the people or spirits involved not to tell people about what He had done (for example, see Mark 1:44).

Although Jesus could have taken any of the many divine titles that were rightfully His, He chose to call Himself "the son of man" during most of His adult ministry (see Mt. 26:63-64).

Jesus could have had an ego, but it wouldn't serve Him. He knew His "ego" would not have been the real Him. Instead,

"And being found in appearance as a man, *He humbled Himself* and *became obedient to the point of death,* even the death of the cross. Therefore *God also has highly exalted Him* and given Him the name which is above every name, that at the name of Jesus every knee should bow, of those in heaven, and of those on earth, and of those under the earth, and that every tongue should confess that Jesus Christ is Lord, to the glory of God the Father" (Phil. 2:8-11, emphasis mine).

That means He declared by His actions and words each day, "My assignment is to come here and die. That is My Father's assignment to Me and that is what I am going to do—nothing more and nothing less."

Satan's Scheme Was to Trick, Badger or Persuade Jesus

The devil knew Jesus Christ was the Son of God. When he approached Jesus in the wilderness, his scheme was to trick, badger, or persuade Jesus to step outside of the Father's requirement that He fulfill His earthly mission as a sinless man instead of as God.

Most of Satan's tactics were probing for any sign in Jesus of the familiar "first Adam image" in the form of human *ego.* Every attempt failed because Jesus refused to step outside of the image of God. "Yes, I am able to do all of these things... I can turn this stone into bread, but it isn't up to Me. Four times Jesus answered Satan's temptations with, *"It is written..."* (see Mt. 4:4, 6-7, 10).

Virtually any Christ-centered local church will grow spiritual light years in a moment if its members leave its four walls with a servant's heart like Jesus, determined to serve one another and those they meet each day.

If I could pinpoint our biggest problem in the typical

Sunday morning congregation—even in the so-called mega churches, it is that we are not as "saved" as we were in previous generations.

"What do you mean, Bishop? Is this some kind of new salvation theology?"

No, we are still saved by faith through the work of Jesus Christ on the cross. The problem is that God doesn't define salvation by mere church attendance or even by acknowledging Him to be the Son of God. It begins with that, but Jesus Himself demanded that we keep *His commandments* if we really love Him.

This sets up some serious problems for people stuck in time with a bad movie running through their minds. Even if 5,000-to-10,000 people show up for a church service, most of the time only 1,000 may actually be "present." The rest of the believers are trapped in continuous thoughts and anxieties about "tomorrow" or replays of "yesterday" memory clips.

Present in the Flesh But Absent in Spirit

These people may clap their hands, sing the songs, or even jump up and down in temporary excitement, but they are not "there." As a result, they can't hear what is being said at the moment—even if the words are pure truth.

This problem with being "present in the flesh but absent in spirit" is serious because whenever God gives you truth, it makes you free. The Bible says, "Now the Lord is the Spirit; and where the Spirit of the Lord is, *there is liberty*" (2 Cor. 3:17, emphasis mine).

The problem is that you have to be "there" in the Spirit to get it. This is the short and simple analysis of our situation on earth:

Yesterday is in the tomb.
Tomorrow is in the womb.
Life is now.

God isn't interested in seeing an army of spiritual zombies showing up in body. He wants your whole heart, your whole mind, your whole spirit, and everything else within you.

I am not pretending to be something I am not. My goal is to be like Jesus, not like my critics or some roving band of bystanders. Nor will I do anything to be like someone else other than Jesus.

It is time to get "unstuck" in time. This is your season to break free of bondage and live in the very image of Christ, but first you must learn to discern between your mind and your spirit (and understand which one is the master of your true identity).

Stop the bad movie from your past and from first Adam's failed image. Enter each new day with your new image in Christ. He has something much better for you:

"Therefore, if anyone is in Christ, he is a new creation; old things have passed away; behold, all things have become new" (2 Cor. 5:17, emphasis mine).

Chapter 8
Whose Mind Is This?

Nearly every week we see news reports about bloody crimes or incredible incidents of abuse and brutality. Unfortunately, we've toughened our emotions so these stories seldom affect us.

The responses of many of the people accused of these crimes are almost as shocking as the crimes themselves. Often they stare blankly into the TV cameras or the faces of law enforcement officials and say, "I don't know why I did it. It just happened I guess...."

Nearly every parent of a teenager has experienced the same response on a less serious scale. "Why did you take the car without permission last night?" Up comes the blank stare with a shrug of the shoulder. "Uh, I dunno. I needed it and you weren't around. So I just took it. It's no big deal."

Most of us know better. Most us understand the consequences too, but we usually cross the line anyway. *Whose* mind is this? What is going on with the human race?

Paul described our sickness nearly 2,000 years ago when he said, "For the flesh lusts against the Spirit, and the Spirit against the flesh; and these are contrary to one another, so that you do not do the things that you wish" (Gal. 5:17).

The Bible says, *"Let this mind be in you which was also in Christ Jesus..."* (Phil. 2:5), but we stay stuck in "the mind which was in Adam."

Christ Jesus had a mind when He was hanging on the cross. He knew He was innocent; He was unjustly accused and condemned to a brutal death. Yet, immediately after He was crucified on a Roman cross between two thieves, at the height of His suffering and pain, He cried out to the Father,

"Father, forgive them, for they do not know what they do" (Luke 23:34).

This is an impossible act in the minds of most church-going people today. Why? Because we are not in His image and we don't have the mind of Christ. We think it is enough to go through the motions in our own mind, but God says, "Let this mind be in you which was also in Christ Jesus."

Is this some kind of "word game" or spiritual metaphor, or is there really a difference between the mind of Christ and the mind of the flesh?

The Works of the Wrong Image are Evident

Paul answered the question with real examples of how these two "minds" work in our lives. He said the "works of the flesh" (the stuff that comes with the wrong image, the image of Adam) are *evident* or openly apparent to everyone. His list appears in Galatians 5:19-21:

- adultery
- fornication
- uncleanness (impure thoughts)
- lewdness (lasciviousness or a hunger for lustful pleasure)
- idolatry
- sorcery (witchcraft or involvement in the occult)
- hatred
- contentions (quarreling with people)
- jealousy
- outbursts of wrath
- selfish ambition
- dissension (division)
- heresy (everyone is wrong except you—including God's Word)
- envy
- murder

- drunkenness
- revelry (wild parties), and the like

Quick Justifications, But No Inheritance

Paul warned us that… "those who practice such things *will not* inherit the Kingdom of God" (Gal. 5:21, emphasis mine). Most of us are quick to justify our fleshly ways by saying, "Well, I haven't committed any murders."

No, but have you committed murder in your mind or heart? "I haven't committed adultery either…" Have you looked at someone with lust in your heart? According to Jesus, if you commit the sin in your heart or mind, then it is the same as if you committed the sin in the flesh (see Mt. 5:28).

The Bible doesn't stop there. Paul moves on to give us a positive list of actions and virtues (the "fruit of the Spirit") that are *evident* or brightly shining and quickly noticed by people looking on from the outside (Gal. 5:22-23). They include:

- love
- joy
- peace
- longsuffering
- kindness
- goodness
- faithfulness
- gentleness
- self-control

Paul said something after giving us this list that should arrest us: He said, "those who are Christ's *have crucified the flesh* with its passions and desires" (Gal. 5:24). It is as if he knew a lot of us would be having problems with our flesh later on, so he put this blunt statement in a place where we couldn't miss it.

DELIVER ME FROM ADAM

104   Finally, Paul said, "If we live in the Spirit, let us also *walk in the Spirit*" (Gal. 5:25, emphasis mine). This is the image of Christ we long for and are called to.

Compromise Produces Instability

We can't do this trying to be somebody else. If the church ever grabs this fact, it will begin to grow up in maturity and effectiveness. Compromise and what the Bible calls "double-mindedness" always produces instability (see Jas. 1:8). As we learned earlier, there are only *two original one-of-a-kind men* ever recorded in the Bible: that's Adam and Christ. Either you're with Adam *and are dead,* or you are in Christ and *alive.* If you are with Christ and alive, then this is *how* you operate. This is His image:

> "Let *nothing* be done through selfish ambition or conceit, but in lowliness of mind let each esteem others better than himself. Let each of you look out not only for his own interests, but also for the interests of others. Let this mind be in you which was also in Christ Jesus..." (Phil. 2:3a-5, emphasis mine).

Ego—the first Adam lingering in our lives—makes us selfish to the core. We may do a good job of disguising it with all of the latest politically correct phrases and justifications ("I take care of Number 1 because no one else is going to..." or "He who gets the most toys wins"), but it is still "self" gratification.

Too many people who call themselves Christians are working primarily to bless, promote, and exalt themselves. They are always trying to build this or do that in the name of productivity. "Yeah, I'm trying to network my way to the top."

Nothing Means "Not Even One"

God says, "Let *nothing* [surprise, the Greek word here

means *"nothing—not even one"*] be done through selfish ambition or conceit, but in lowliness of mind let each esteem others better than himself" (Phil. 2:3a).[1]

You and I both know we have our own minds. But the million-dollar question is, "Whose mind is this?"

It is time to stop all pretending and end our attempts to be what we are not. Jesus warned believers in the church at Laodicea to either be hot or be cold, but He would spit out anyone who tried to live in compromise and be lukewarm in their Christian life (see Rev. 3:15-16).

It doesn't matter whether I occupy the position of bishop and appear on national television or am buying food at my local grocery store—God expects me to be the same person and spread the same godly light all of the time. He is sick of watching us masquerade our false religion as if we are on parade in public while living a lie in private. We need to get comfortable with who we are in Christ.

Once again, the problems of the mind cannot be solved on the level of the mind. Every human problem must be solved from a higher level than what it is formed in. You always have to reach higher than where you are to get pulled out of what you are in.

Reach Beyond the Limited Resources of Your Mind

The mind cannot comprehend or execute what God has ordained. That means you and I must reach beyond the limited resources and powers of the mind and reach into the Spirit to fulfill our destiny and live in Christ.

The only way we will ever figure this out and live it out is to let God bring it in! Jesus put it this way:

"I am the vine, you are the branches. He who *abides in Me,* and I in him, *bears much fruit; for without Me you can do nothing.* If anyone does not abide in

Me, he is cast out as a branch and is withered; and they gather them and throw them into the fire, and they are burned. *If you abide in Me,* and My words abide in you, you will ask what you desire, and it shall be done for you. By this My Father is glorified, *that you bear much fruit;* so you will be My disciples" (John 15:5-8, emphasis mine).

Too many of us run off to live life our own way saying, "Well, Jesus accepted me just as I am," not realizing that God's will is to conform us to be "just as He is." Just as I am just isn't good enough. We are saved to be *conformed* to someone greater than we are (see Rom. 8:29, 12:2).

One of the biggest problems we have is our inner urge to somehow be "unique." Actually, we are making the same mistake Eve made in the Garden of Eden. Adam and Eve had already been created in the image and likeness of God, but they believed the serpent's lies and sinned, hoping to be like God.

We Forfeit the Divine Image by Looking Outside of God

That quality or divine image was already there, but they forfeited it when they tried to find meaning outside of their relationship with God.

The image of the first Adam tries to be unique. The image of Christ, the last Adam, already is unique, but its only ambition is to be what God ordained. When you "give up your life" to receive Christ, He in turn gives you "life, and that more abundantly."

God says, in essence, "I am not trying to get you to be unique (I already made you that way). I am trying to get you to be Me! If you are connected to Me, I am going to think through you. If you are not connected to Me, then I am going to cut you off, you are going to whither, and die spiritually."

Remember that in Adam, all things die. In Christ, all
things are made alive. Adam became a living being, but Christ
became a life-giving spirit. If you are in Christ, then you have
become a life-giving spirit. We are in Christ, therefore, we live.

Our whole thought process must be delivered, which
brings us full circle to the question, "Whose mind is this?"

You Choose: Death or Life?

The goal of all of this is simple: to move us from living in
the death-dealing image of the first Adam to living through
the life-giving image of the last Adam, Jesus Christ.

No matter what you do and no matter how many
accolades, trophies, plaques, banquets or pats on the back you
get—you still have to ask yourself the question: "Whose mind
is this?"

If you live in the image of the last Adam, then you won't
rely primarily on your five senses for direction and guidance in
life. You will *walk by faith and not by sight* (see 2 Cor. 5:7).

It is God's design to prosper you and set you apart from the
world by *what you see in the Spirit,* not by what you see or do
not see in the physical and natural realm. He gets all of the
glory when we dare to call things out of the invisible into the
visible realm. That is simply operating in the image of God.

It is sad to see so many born-again Christians living—or
existing I should say—in the dim and fallen image of Adam.
The reason so many of us go through life broken down, torn
down, talking down, and thinking down, is because we are
locked in the box of our five physical senses.

We are eternal spirits deprived of true sight, hearing, and
spiritual perception as long as we remain locked in this box of
flesh! The saddest part of this picture is that God has given us
the key to unlock and walk out of that box forever. God is
saying, *"Walk in the Spirit!"*

108   Most of the things we think are our problems aren't really ours—they belong to our adversary. Too often, however, we see them and accept them as our own.

Distracted by False Readings From the Five Senses

We never see most of the things that sabotage our lives. Why? Much of the time we are distracted by false readings from our five natural senses. (It might be different if we could manage to spend more than five minutes in our devotions each day....)

God has a way of speaking to you and alarming your spirit when you are somewhere that you shouldn't be. He also encourages and brings peace to your spirit when you are where you are supposed to be (see Phil. 4:6-7, Col. 3:15).

When you are where you are supposed to be, you can look at somebody and say, "It's good for us to be here." But when you're not where you are supposed to be, something just doesn't feel right. It doesn't matter how pretty everything looks or how impressive a place or event seems, something just isn't right. If you are wise, you will simply say, *"See ya!"*

The Bible says, "And let the peace of God rule in your hearts, to which also you were called in one body; and be thankful" (Col. 3:15). The Amplified Bible tells us there is much more to the original Greek word for "rule" than most English translations imply.

> **"And let the peace (soul harmony which comes) from Christ rule *(act as umpire continually)* in your hearts *[deciding and settling with finality all questions that arise in your minds,* in that peaceful state] to which as [members of Christ's] one body you were also called [to live]..."** (Col. 3:15, AMP, italics mine).[2]

Nothing Has Changed, Nothing is New

If you never make the shift to live in Christ rather than

in Adam, then you still don't know who you are. When you ask yourself the question, "Whose mind is this?" you get the disappointing answer: "It is the same old mind and broken image I've been dragging around from the beginning. Nothing has changed and nothing is new."

Only two paths are left at that point—either you do things God's way or you create your own false image of "a somebody." Then you go through life disguised in the thin veneer of a false identity called your ego. This self-made image patterned after Adam and whatever happens to be politically correct at the time is easily bruised, crushed, or manipulated by fear and rejection.

Again, the definition of dying in Christ is that God strips away from you everything that is not you. He takes away the trappings of the first Adam to make room for the eternal reality of the last Adam.

Now don't assume that God does this politely. It is as if He removes a baby bottle that we have been sucking on all of our lives—we are likely to have tantrums just as we did when we were children! We take our toys and run when correction comes! (Almost everybody has a song about a church or church leader that hurt them.)

What if you did everything God asks in His Word? You have "died to self" and lived unto Christ. You have based your identity and eternal worth on His love and sacrifice for you, not in your works, reputation, or status among your peers. You now exert more effort looking out for and esteeming others, rather than seeking approval and affirmation for yourself.

Conditioned and Positioned by the Fallen World

If all of this is true, then how did your feelings get hurt while you were esteeming everybody more than yourself?

The answer is that we *are not comfortable being like Christ.*

110 We are conditioned and positioned by the fallen world to become what Adam and Eve wanted in the garden—to be "individuals" having a destiny separate from God.

Most of us try to hide the fact that we really do not want to be called "real holy." Even though God commands that we be holy just as He is, we put more weight on the disapproval of our peers than on the approval of our God.

We give lip service to being "holy," but we dread the day somebody sees us in the mall or at work and says with a sneer to anyone who will listen, "O-h-h-h, there goes that *real holy* girl."

"Uh, I ain't *that* holy."

Why do you instinctively make a defensive statement or partial denial? The true motive is that you don't want that label. It hurts when friends disapprove of you. Your friends may not want to meet with you or invite you to lunch. They might even cut you out of their inner circle (and you have to admit that you desperately want to be cut in).

"I'm Trying to Protect My Image"

The only honest evaluation of our actions is that we have to deny Christ each day if we want to win our friends approval and be affirmed according to their values. "I have to be luke-warm, because I'm trying to *protect* my image." Whose mind is this?

There is only one way to heaven, and there is only one way we can walk in power and dominion—we must enter God's Kingdom through Jesus the door, and we must rule the earth in *His* image.

That only happens as you allow *Him* to take away from you everything that is *not* you so that the old you dies. The whole secret of life is for you to die before you die so you know you don't have to die (more on this later).

One of the clearest pictures of the way God transforms your life is found in the oldest book of the Bible. The book of

Job describes the life of a righteous man blessed with large herds of livestock, a large family, and a great fortune.

One day every earthly possession that appeared to "make" Job was taken away—even his health. What was Job's response?

"And he said: 'Naked I came from my mother's womb, and naked shall I return there. The LORD gave, and the LORD has taken away; blessed be the name of the LORD.' In all this Job did not sin nor charge God with wrong" (Job 1:21-22).

We Totally Miss the Gold Hidden Within

Most people in America today think people are "what they have." That is why so many people seeking marriage partners in the church have bypassed their intended spouses. God usually shows them to us in a "stripped down" form (Job style). As long as we walk and live in the box of our physical senses, we write off people who don't have "stuff" and totally miss the gold hidden within.

God illustrated a truth for us in His oldest book: Job had a revelation when God took away every material possession from him and stripped him down to nothing.

"When I first came in here with nothing, I was still somebody. I am going out of here with nothing, but I will still be somebody. So the 'nothing' isn't what makes me. What makes me is this unchanging confession of my heart: 'Blessed be the name of the Lord.'

That is what makes me. My worth isn't built on the foundation of my wealth, my house, my livestock, or my health. It isn't even based on the lives and well-being of my children—they are gifts from God, not possessions I own. I am something because He is everything. Blessed be the name of the Lord."

At every stage of life, we should ask ourselves, *"Whose mind is this?"* When you feel depression creeping over you, ask the question. When an irritating or vicious person ignites anger and hostility in your heart, ask the question. When you feel overwhelmed by the shortcomings or failures that are bound to show up, ask the question.

If you come up with the wrong answer, then make the right decision then and there. "If anyone sins, we have an advocate with the Father, Jesus Christ the righteous" (1 John 2:1b).

End Notes

1. Strong, *Strong's Exhaustive Concordance of the Bible,* Greek—3367. medeis, may-dice'; includ. the irreg. fem. medemia, may-dem-ee'-ah, and the neut. meden, may-den'; from G3361 and G1520; *not even one* (man, woman, thing): –any (man, thing), no (man), none, not (at all, any man, a whit), *nothing,* + without delay [emphasis mine].

2. *The Amplified Bible,* Expanded Edition (Grand Rapids, MI: Zondervan, by permission of The Lockman Foundation, 1987), p. 1393.

Chapter 9
God Wants You To Live

God wants to deliver you from flesh to spirit. This is the good news.

The bad news is that you must die to self.

"What do you mean?"

It is the only way God can save you. The only way you can claim life in Christ is to give up your life in Adam's image.

Jesus said, "And he who does not take his cross [a tool to help you die] and follow after Me is not worthy of Me. He who finds his life will lose it, and he who loses his life for My sake will find it" (Mt. 10:38-39).

How do we lose our lives for His sake? The first way seems to be martyrdom, but Jesus also taught that this takes place on a *daily* basis, so He was talking about a gradual dying process. The first step is to repent or turn away from our fallen life in Adam's image, receive Him as Lord and Savior, then follow Him the rest of our lives.

The second step is much more difficult—and it lasts a lifetime. This is where we "die daily" on the cross we carry (see Luke 9:23). The dying part comes as you allow Him (through the Holy Spirit) to strip away everything that is not really you. Just as soon as you think it's safe to drop the cross and move on, the Lord takes you in a new direction and reminds you that it is time to remove more dead stuff so more of Him can shine through you.

Three examples in nature may illustrate the importance of God's "death unto life" process in Christ.

• Butterflies begin life as a larva or worm-like creature. The larva weaves a protective cocoon and undergoes a

114 transformation called metamorphosis. Only by breaking through the cocoon will the new butterfly emerge. If it remains in the protective cocoon, it dies.

• In the "fullness of time," a baby chick inside the egg begins to peck frantically at its imprisoning shell. What once served as its outer shell and shield from the outside world is now a deadly barrier, blocking its future and potentially dooming it to premature death. Even the process of struggling to pierce the shell, and then to emerge from its fragile birth-place strengthens and prepares the chick for success in a newer, higher realm of a larger world.

• Approximately nine months from conception, a human baby has reached the end of its life in the womb and must begin a transformation of its own. Up until that point, all of the baby's needs—its oxygen, fluids, food, waste evacuation, and body temperature—have been supplied or regulated by Mama. Now it moves into a head-down position for its most difficult and most dangerous journey in human life. It must move out of the protective womb and into the narrow birth canal. Its journey through the canal takes it through a small passage in the mother's pelvic bone structure and into the new world outside.

If the baby remains in the womb too long, all of the support structures begin to pull away from the mother's body or cease to function. Babies are destined to be born and enter the greater world outside the womb, not remain hidden forever. The former is called birth. The latter is called "still-birth" or spontaneous abortion.

Die Before You Die

In each example, the new life within dies if the old does not fully "fall away" or transform. This is the heart of the "secret of life." You must "die before you die," and only then do you discover that there is no death for those in Christ. The old must be removed before the new is fully revealed.

"And being found in appearance as a man, He 115 *humbled Himself* and *became obedient to the point of death,* even the death of the cross. Therefore, *God also has highly exalted Him* and *given Him the name* which is above every name..." (Phil. 2:8-9, emphasis mine).

Jesus was saying with words and deeds, "I am not trying to force My will; I want My Father's will. If I must die, then that is My course." He was willing to lay down His life and pick up the agenda of God.

The pattern of death unto life is just as important for us today as it was for Jesus 2,000 years ago. First Jesus *humbled* Himself. It is not God's job to humble you—it is yours. The Bible says, "God resists the proud, but gives grace to the humble." Therefore humble yourselves under the mighty hand of God, that He may exalt you in due time" (1 Pet. 5:5b-6).

Second, He became *obedient* to the Father, even though it required Him to die. Jesus calls you to pick up your cross and follow Him. If you are obedient, then the first Adam nature that held you in bondage will die and the image of Christ will give you life.

Thirdly, God *exalted* Him after He made Himself low (of no reputation). Fourth, God *gave Him a name.* This is where you and I should get our reputations and learn our true name.

Immune to Attractions, Distractions, and Disapproval

If you live and operate in the Spirit, then you shouldn't be intimidated by what other people say and do. The life of Christ in you should make you immune to the attractions, distractions, and disapproval of other people.

The problem is that we have been conditioned to expect shortcuts, cheat codes, fast service, bargain prices, and special treatment in life. God offers and honors none of these. He honors people who allow themselves to be conformed to the image of His Son through love, obedience, sacrifice, humility, perseverance, patience, and holiness.

Do you ever watch people when you go downtown or visit a large metro center? I have seen people who walk around talking to themselves. Most of us would label them "crazy" (the politically correct term would be "mentally impaired").

Honestly, I think we might be just as crazy as they are because we do the same thing—only we don't do it out loud! In our version of insanity, we sit there talking back and forth with our ego.

We tell ourselves (even though no one else is there) how awful the person is who just walked by without saying hello in the church building, or what a hypocrite Mrs. Whatsit is for not inviting us to her dinner party, or why we are better than most of the other people in the church because we tithed on our gambling winnings the week before.

Adam Causes us to Forget Weightier Matters

God wants to destroy the first Adam in us that masquerades as the last Adam because it causes us to forget or dismiss the "weightier matters" of justice, mercy, and faith" while focusing on unimportant matters centered on self (see Mt. 23:23).

"The air is too cold in here." "No, it's way too hot in here."

"That woman took *my* chair. I've been sittin' in that chair since the new preacher came some thirty years ago. Who does she think she is?"

"No, he is not my brother. He doesn't believe like I do. That boy will eat almost anything! It can't be right. No matter what you say, he can't be going to the same heaven I'm goin' to."

"Now you just don't understand—those rules don't apply to me. I'm a deacon, you see."

"What do you mean I can't do that...I'm an elder and elders don't..."

No, you don't understand that when you claim to be a man **117** or woman of God, then you are called to be a *servant*. When we dodge those lingering thoughts of the cross and cling to our old Adam nature, then we end up just too arrogant; too nasty and too crazy to truly represent our holy Savior.

We have disregarded God's direct commands in favor of listening to the devious whisperings of that "little buddy" sitting on our shoulders. (Adam and Eve had the serpent; we have the "little buddy" of our own invention.)

No Dying, No Life

Listen: that ego-driven, self-centered voice you are hearing isn't you. If there is no dying, then there is no life.

Rejection—that gnawing feeling that hits you when you are made an outcast because of your commitment to be like Jesus—is one of the most feared by-products of "dying to self" on the cross of Christ.

Of all our fears, this one has the most reality behind it. Sometimes it is lonely when you are pursuing godliness. Even Paul the apostle warned us that, *"...all who desire to live godly in Christ Jesus will suffer persecution"* (2 Tim. 3:12, emphasis mine). This deep sense of "aloneness" may be one of the biggest challenges facing members of contemporary, charismatic-style churches today.

It seems that most of us will admit to feeling lonely on certain days—even leaders.

Sometimes I can sense my "buddy," my ego, trying to talk me into depression and loneliness. My most vulnerable moments seem to come when I am physically alone or by myself for long periods. In weak moments, I used to allow my ego to become "me" and I immediately started looking at folk differently. All of that has to die and be left at the cross.

Why do we feel so alone? Jesus said:

"Most assuredly, I say to you, *unless a grain of wheat falls into the ground and dies,* it remains alone; but if it dies, it produces much grain. He who loves his life will lose it, and he who hates his life in this world will keep it for eternal life" (John 12:24-25, emphasis mine.).

Adam Must Die

We are alone because we live in the first Adam, and that old man has an appointment with the grave. The principle Jesus revealed in John's gospel applies equally well to the image of the first Adam. "Most assuredly, I say to you, *unless Adam falls into the ground and dies,* you will remain alone, but if the first Adam dies, then the last Adam in you will produce much fruit."

"Well, Bishop, that only applies to Jesus and the cross." No, it applies to *all* of us. The sixth chapter of Romans describes how "our old man"—the first Adam nature in us —dies and what happens in the process.

"How shall we who died to sin live any longer in it? Or *do you not know* that as many of us as were *baptized into Christ* Jesus were *baptized unto His death?* Therefore *we were buried with Him* through baptism into death, that j*ust as Christ was raised from the dead* by the glory of the Father, *even so we also should walk in newness of life.* For if we have been united together in the likeness of His death, certainly we also shall be in the likeness of His resurrection, knowing this, that *our old man* was *crucified with Him, that the body of sin might be done away with, that we should no longer be slaves of sin.* For he who has died has been freed from sin" (Rom. 6:2-7, emphasis mine).

You will always feel alone unless you die to your Adam-based self-image and take on the image of Christ. The Bible asks, "Do you not know…?"

You know the feeling…you leave the house just moments before a final touchdown attempt in a football game or the last scene in a dramatic movie—and then return seconds *after it's all over!* When you ask about the outcome, you get the predictable replies, "You mean you don't know? You haven't heard? Oh…you missed it!"

The Deed is Done—the Old Man is Dead

That is the situation being relayed to the Christians in Rome (and to us). Our "old man" has already been killed. The deed is done; the first Adam's body has already been crucified on the cross with Jesus Christ. Now we are trying to catch up to what we missed.

The themes of death, crucifixion, and burial appear continuously in the book of Romans. Why? It is because they are absolutely linked to life in Christ. It is written, "Now if we died with Christ, we believe that we shall also live with Him" (Rom. 6:8).

What does this mean? How can we "die" with Christ and then live with Him? We find a simple and direct answer to our questions in Paul's letter to the Colossians:

"In Him you were also circumcised with the circumcision made without hands, by *putting off the body of the sins of the flesh,* by the circumcision of Christ, *buried with Him in baptism,* in which you also were *raised with Him through faith* in the working of God, who raised Him from the dead. And you, being dead in your trespasses and the uncircumcision of your flesh, He has made alive together with Him, having forgiven you all trespasses" (Col. 2:11-13, emphasis mine).

Play a Crucial Part in Your Death

While it is true that God wants you to die to your own selfish ambitions, it is also true that you have a crucial part to play in bringing it to pass. The book of Romans says: "For if you live according to the flesh you will die; but *if by the Spirit you put to death the deeds of the body,* you will live" (Rom. 8:13, emphasis mine).

Do you see God's perfect love motive behind His desire for you to live the abundant life? This is how it is summed up in Romans:

"Likewise you also, reckon yourselves to be *dead indeed to sin,* but *alive to God in Christ Jesus our Lord.* Therefore *do not let sin reign* in your mortal body, that you should obey it in its lusts. And do not present your members as instruments of unrighteousness to sin, but present yourselves to God as being alive from the dead, and your members as instruments of righteousness to God. *For sin shall not have dominion over you, for you are not under law but under grace"* (Rom. 6:11-14, emphasis mine).

People who insist on dragging their old Adam image in and out of church, into the workplace, and all around their neighborhoods actually work for Satan and against Christ. In other words, they exalt satan's agenda through selfish ambition.

What Are You Lifting Up Before Others?

Ask yourself, "What am *I* lifting up before others?" Jesus said, "And I, if I am lifted up from the earth, will *draw all peoples* to Myself" (John 12:32, emphasis mine). When we allow Christ to live through us, we exalt God's agenda.

Virtually the whole twelfth chapter of John concerns itself with the death of self, the burial of self, and resurrection in

Christ. Once again, the example of Christ's deeds on the cross **121** set an example for us in our daily lives.

If this view is wrong, then why would Jesus say (and we mentioned earlier), "If anyone desires to come after Me, let him deny *himself,* and take up his cross daily, and follow Me" (Luke 9:23)? Now apply the principle Jesus established in Luke to His prophetic words in John 12:

> **"And I, if I die to self as Jesus died; and allow the Christ in me to be lifted up from the earth on the cross of obedience, then I, too, will *draw all peoples* to the Christ in me."**

If you lift up and publicly display the self-centered, double-minded and compromising image of Adam to the people with whom you live and work, you will "draw" the same kind of people to yourself!

For example, I can't tell you how many times I've heard single adults moan about the difficulties of the "single's scene." It is true that life as a single adult in today's immoral culture can be very difficult, but many of the people I've heard cry the loudest created their own problems.

"Why is it I always meet crazy people?"

What Image Do You Project at Work?

The business realm and the workplace are other areas that seem to accurately reflect the quality of spiritual life we "lift up" or project before others. Hundreds of people have received business training through skilled business leaders and ministers in our church.

Why? They found that many secular universities, business schools, and career advancement institutes teach a little more than how to rationally analyze and manipulate people. The techniques taught seem to rely exclusively upon the five natural

122 senses (excluding any spiritual insight or perception) and a virtually nonexistent foundation of ethics and moral conviction.

"You need to write this kind of memo to protect yourself."

"Don't bother with these reports—the government will never know and the company accountant will never ask."

"Recommend these stocks often—they pay you a higher commission (...and don't worry about actual payback to the customer. You get paid by the number of transactions; not by whether they actually work or not)."

"Make sure you build and maintain a negative file on your competition in the office...you're gonna need it."

"Above all, make sure you keep those kickback payouts going to the customers and vendors. As long as you do that, you can stay on top. But as soon as you stop, you are going to fall."

Show up Looking Like Me

According to the principle established by Christ's example, God says: *If you can show up at work looking like Me and blessing others as I would, then you will be promoted to the head of the table. If you can show up at work looking, serving, and thinking like Me, then I will expose the plots of anyone who tries to destroy you.*

If you and I can wake up tomorrow morning with our hearts focused on God's Kingdom and His righteous way of living, loving, and serving, He promises to send people into our paths who will assist us in meeting our needs. (see Mt. 6:33).

I've noticed over many years of ministry that if a man or woman desiring a godly spouse begins looking and acting like Jesus, the Christ in them somehow *draws* the right person into their lives!

When God is doing the matchmaking, and when you stay busy lifting *Him* up in your life, then you don't have to worry about looking "sexy" to land your life partner. I am convinced

you could put on a body-length burlap sack and He would **123**
still send the right one into your life!

You don't have to settle for second-best either. Based on the principles revealed in God's Word, He would tell you, essentially, "I have somebody for you, but he or she can't come after *you;* they must be drawn to the *Me* revealed in you. This is for your blessing and protection."

You and I must get the right image—Christ's image. "And I, *if I am lifted up* from the earth, will *draw all* peoples to Myself" (John 12:32, emphasis mine). The right hookups in relationships, vocation, and ministry rarely if ever come in your life when *you* are in charge. If you are tired of attracting all of the wrong people for all of the wrong reasons, pray this prayer with me

> *Search me O God, if there be anything in me that is not like You—remove it so I can become the person and example You have ordained for me to be. Rise up in me, Lord. If trouble comes my way, I yield to and trust You to remove it from my life. Be glorified in my life, Lord Jesus. Amen.*

Chapter 10
How to Start Over

There are times when the only way to start over is to really "start over." The old must pass away completely before beginning with the new.

Jesus warned about putting new wine into old wineskins, knowing He had come in the flesh to be God's living fresh start for humanity. He said, "No one puts new wine into old wineskins; or else the new wine bursts the wineskins, the wine is spilled, and the wineskins are ruined. But new wine must be put into new wineskins" (Mark 2:22).

If you start writing a letter with a pen or pencil, there are times when mistakes or a wrong beginning forces you to start over with a clean sheet of paper.

The computer age brought countless changes in our lives. One is the ability to instantly backtrack and delete mistakes in documents. Even so, there are times when it is best to start over with a blank page or a new document.

When I prepare to create a written masterpiece on my computer, I hit "WORD"[1] and a new clean page comes to the screen in front of me. This cybernetic version of a clean sheet of paper represents a fresh start in more ways than one.

In the real-life realm of the spirit, whenever we pull up *Word*—God's unchanging and eternal Word empowered by Christ's work on the cross, our repentance, and a desire for a new beginning—we get the ultimate clean slate for the soul and spirit!

All previous marks, erasures, and evidence in the soul of past mistakes, errors, acts of stupidity, and overt sin are wiped out (including the marks of lust, poverty, abuse, hatred, and

126 even murder). God wants you and I to be free!

Once I act on God's Word and allow Him to erase and delete my past mistakes and sins through the blood of Jesus Christ, then I can start over.

All of my sins and failures are forgiven and the very record of their existence is destroyed. The image of the first Adam disappears and all God the Father sees in me is the image of His Son! I have become "a totally new document" on God's "computer."

Plant Pruning and Computer Viruses

Our heavenly Father *prunes* the branches of His vine from time to time (that means *us*) to make us more fruitful and productive (see John 15:1-6). That means He cuts off or trims away dead and unproductive things from our lives.

If you are caught up in the things He is trimming away— the pleasures of the world, the pride of life, the sins you know you should be avoiding—then you may miss what He wants to produce through your life.

If we shift to computer terminology, sin and Adam's image are essentially fatal computer "bugs" or viruses that *will* absolutely corrupt your life. God loves you so much that He will remove those viruses, even if it seems He must let you die to self to do it.

Yes, your "computer" may have been crippled or nearly destroyed by Adam's fatal virus, but the *real you* is still there, hidden in Christ. You have to get rid of the Adam virus, or it will infect and contaminate every new page and every new day of your life!

- New wine, new wineskin.
- Prune the vine, get a more fruitful vine.
- Remove the virus, load new software from a totally new source, and reboot the computer for a brand new start.

- Lose your life in Adam, receive new life in Christ **127**

"Well, Bishop, how do I stop the virus of "Adam's image" from infecting my life?" The answer is clear and simple: *"Therefore, if anyone is in Christ, he is a new creation; old things have passed away; behold, all things have become new"* (2 Cor. 5:17). To begin again, you must:

1. Eradicate the old image of Adam under the blood of Jesus.
2. "Download" God's custom-written operating system— the image of Christ, "sealed" in blood.
3. Begin again as a new creature in a new divine image.

"GIGO" was one of the first words created by early programming pioneers of the computer world. It is an acronym for "Garbage In, Garbage Out." In other words, what you say and do *outwardly* reveals what is *inside* you.

For centuries, Christians have tried to pretend that what they thought about or focused on in their daily lives wouldn't affect their faith in God.

The Apostle Paul bluntly confronted this error in his letter to the Colossians. (Avoid the temptation to skip past this scripture citation. The extra effort to read it will *empower you* to live in victory and avoid defeat!):

"Set your *mind* on things above, not on things on the earth. For *you died,* and *your life is hidden with Christ in God.* When Christ who is our life appears, then you also will appear with Him in glory. Therefore *put to death your members* which are on the earth [(NLT) "the sinful, earthly things lurking within you"— (NIV) "whatever belongs to your earthly nature"]: fornication, uncleanness, passion, evil desire, and covetousness, which is idolatry. Because of these things the wrath of God is coming upon the sons of disobedience, in which you yourselves once walked when you lived in them. But now *you yourselves are to put off* all these: anger, wrath, malice, blasphemy, filthy language out of your mouth. Do not lie to one another, since *you have put off the old man* with his deeds, and have *put on the new man* who is renewed in knowledge *according to the image of Him* who created him" (Col. 3:2-10, emphasis mine).

The real apostle said, *"now you yourself are to...."* The ball is in your court. If you feed garbage to your mind and soul, then don't be surprised if garbage shows up in almost every area of your life.

The GIGO principle existed long before the first computer was invented. It was Jesus who said in His Word, "Out of the abundance of the heart the mouth speaks" (Mt. 12:34, Luke 6:45).

Many years ago, I was a single parent raising my oldest son, Eric. He came up during the era of a pop group called New Edition.

Every morning Eric would put on one particular album by that group. In fact, four of his closest friends did the same thing. When the boys got home from school every afternoon, they listened to that album again and again, memorizing the words, singing the tunes, and practicing the dance steps. The process was repeated every night.

He Was No Longer Himself—it Scared Me

One day I woke up and saw that Eric had actually *become* just like one of the members of New Edition. I am not kidding! He still looked like Eric, but his spirit, his conversation, and his mannerisms had all radically changed. He was no longer himself. It scared me.

Some spirit had overtaken Eric to the point that I had to break the record and refocus him. All of the boys had come to believe they were the group! It was long past being a joke; it was a serious thing. Why did it happen? It happened because they *meditated* on being like New Edition day and night until they literally became what they meditated on— and they didn't even know they had changed!

Do you remember what the Apostle John said about seeing Jesus? He wrote:

> **"Beloved, now we are children of God; and it has not yet been revealed what we shall be, but we know that when He is revealed, we shall be like Him, for we *shall* see Him as He is" (1 John 3:2, emphasis mine).**

This is a divine principle that says we become what we envision. That is why the Bible warns us, "Where there is no vision, the people perish..." (Prov. 29:18a, KJV).

It is basically saying that if you fail to get a revelation of God, you will die. If you get a revelation or focus your vision on anything or anyone other than God, you will "become" that thing. And that process ends in death.

When you meditate on something, it can begin to dominate or control your thoughts. Whether you realize it or not, you will gradually *become* that upon which you are meditating. That is why we need to be careful about where we put our focus and interest.

When I grew up, the top television shows were "Leave it to Beaver," "Father Knows Best," "The Lawrence Welk Show," "Bozo the Clown," and the early black and white versions of "The Mickey Mouse Club." Every family had a mom *and* a dad with children, and the father always worked.

This is Progress?

We have "progressed" since then. Every television program is in color, and most of the situation comedies project fractured families with one spouse gone or in active adultery, with severely dysfunctional relationships, or with openly gay family members and relationships. Plus, there are twisted music videos available virtually around the clock. (Yet, most of us say nothing about it. We write no letters, direct no phone calls, and make no protests.)

We claim to be Christians (Christ-like ones), but somehow we think that something mystical will happen because we graciously manage to "bless the Lord" by showing up for Sunday and Wednesday services (or maybe just the Sunday morning service on "busy" weekends).

Our part-time commitments to God only reflect our shallowness and impotent faith. If you want to know what you really represent, to your family and your unsaved friends or coworkers, then evaluate what you meditate upon day and night.

A long time ago I accepted the truth about my preaching. No matter how wonderful I may be as a preacher and teacher of God's Word, most folks will walk away from my messages unchanged! Why? The Word changes us in direct proportion to the depth it takes root in our souls (examine the Lord's "parable of the sower" in Luke 8:5-15 if you doubt me).

Meditate Upon and Do God's Word

If the only time you hear or receive the Word is when it is preached or taught in a church service, then you will never benefit fully from the power in God's promises! That only comes when you meditate upon and *do* His Word.

To the best of my ability, I do not preach what I have read, I preach what I am *becoming*. Too many people jump from church to church, complaining, "The preacher isn't deep enough." The truth is that the real responsibility for searching out and receiving God's Word to the point of transformation *is with you.*

None of us will be transformed if all we do is show up for church services twice a week. The only way to "chew" and fully digest spiritual food is to *meditate* upon it.

The Bible talks about meditating on God's Word and commandments (26 times in the *New King James Version* to be exact). You can turn to Psalm 1, Deuteronomy 28, or to one gospel and two apostolic letters in the New Testament.[2] It is still the same principle.

God offered this advise to one of His champions about to face a dangerous challenge:

> "This Book of the Law shall not depart from your mouth, but *you shall meditate in it day and night,* that you may *observe to do* according to all that is written in it. For then you will make your way *prosperous,* and then you will have good success" (Josh. 1:8, emphasis mine).

This is No Bellybutton and Floor Mat Word

Most of us hear the word "meditate" and we think of omeone in a robe or yoga outfit contemplating his or her navel on a floor mat. The Hebrew word for meditate is no "belly-button and floor mat" word. It actually means to murmur (in pleasure or anger), ponder, imagine, meditate, mourn, mutter, roar, speak, study, talk, or utter.[3]

God expects you and I to mutter what He says day and night! We need to be muttering it, roaring it, speaking it, murmuring it, pondering it, imagining it, speaking it, studying it, talking about it, and uttering it continually. It seems to me there is no way out—we are to be consumed and obsessed with God's Word.

He also commands us to *observe* His Word. That means you are to build a hedge of thorns around it, guard it, protect it, and attend to it. It also means you must beware, be circumspect, take heed, keep, mark, look narrowly, observe, preserve, regard, reserve, save, make sure, wait for, and watch over it.[4]

God says, "Study My Word, ponder it, speak it, shout it, get it in you and then observe it. Guard what you're studying." When you build a thorny hedge of protection around the promises and commands of God, then anyone or anything that tries to touch, steal, or hinder what you have from God is going to "get wrecked and torn up."

Honestly, we give our minds too much liberty. Every time a new movie comes out, church people go to it. It doesn't matter that the content of the film kills, steals and destroys what God's Word says to behold. We still go "because everybody else goes."

Let Nothing Override or Set Aside God's Word!

If you are a single Christian, and you go to movies that glorify adultery, then you are going to have trouble walking a straight walk. Refuse to allow anything in your mind or emotions that will override or set aside what God has said!

The same thing goes for music ("Uh oh, there goes Bishop messing with my personal stuff again"). There are good songs and bad songs. Don't say, "Oh, I'm just listening to the beat" when the artist is actually cussing you out "to the beat." You might be listening to "the beat" but your mind is downloading the messages from hell in those lyrics. (If you do it anyway, don't wonder why you aren't successful.)

The Psalmist said, "Your word have I hidden in my heart that I might not sin against you" (Ps. 119:11). God gave you a mind as a *tool* to protect what He has given you to meditate upon. If you follow through and meditate on His Word, then you will be prosperous.

The Lord is talking about far more than the balance in your checking account. When God makes you prosperous, you have the power to push forward, break out, become mighty, go over, be good, be equal to, and to be profitable.[5]

Spiritual Junk Food Soaked In Doubt, Unbelief and Selfishness

Our problem is that we think our way out of being prosperous. Most saints are tired because they feed on spiritual junk food soaked in doubt, unbelief, and selfishness.

God says those who meditate on His Word will have *success*. God's definition of success has nothing to do with Gucci, Mercedes Benz, Tommy Boy, or the Trump Towers.

If I have godly success, it means I have the ability to look around and be cautious, to consider all circumstances, possibilities, and consequences. It means I am prudent, marked by wisdom, and practical in my affairs. I am skillful, having understanding and wisdom.[5]

Unfortunately, that kind of definition of a "Bible word" really messes up some churches. Why? It is because those words just don't sound very spiritual.

I've learned that if you have to deal with a bank, then you shouldn't plan to go into the bank president's office talking in tongues or offering mini-sermons and religious platitudes. Believe me, you will walk out of there with nothing.

On the other hand, if you walk in God's success, you will have prepared yourself with skilled entrepreneurial training and a solid business proposal under your arm. You will have proof that you understand your business or ministry expansion plan from front to back. You have studied the consequences, demographics, and probabilities enough to be a genuine expert on the matter.

Don't trot into a banker's office or city hall poorly prepared and clothed in religious ignorance.

"Well, the Lord said you were gonna give me some money and the deed to the land I need. Bishop So and So said there was gonna be a breakthrough and I'm here waitin' for you to breakthrough."

"Do you have a job and steady income?"

"I'm gonna get that, too, but right now I'm believing this is my property. O-h-h, I felt something...."

"Well, I don't know what you felt; but I do know that you can leave my office. If you can't pay and qualify, then neither the money nor the land is yours."

God is practical. Who knows how many Christians have failed in business because they thought they heard God say, "You are a businessperson." They never *studied* to show themselves approved in the Word or in the "business" they were supposed to have.

Building On a "Shonda" and Money From Wanda

Many people think that speaking in tongues is all they need to do to get the things they desire. "I'm going to build a business on a 'shonda' while borrowing money from Wanda." No, they will not be successful because they failed to make God's Word real in their lives by *meditating* upon and *guarding* His Word in their lives.

God commanded Joshua to meditate on His Word because it is the only way to place it *deep* inside the heart where it becomes automatic and authoritative. People generally don't like anything that sounds like work or labor.

Shallow belief is only a heartbeat away from unbelief. In a nutshell, as long as we've been saved and as long as the Word of God has been written, most of us still don't believe it. What a sad commentary on the modern church. We think and act as if the Bible is little more than a somehow holy but completely outdated history book. We study and mediate on everything else but the Bible—car repair manuals, home decorating magazines, computer and videogame manuals.

If you want to start over and make it count, you have to do more than dance your way up the aisles of the church or attend all of the latest classes and fellowship meetings.

Simply "Be" What You Already Are by Faith

The only way to *be* like Christ is to meditate on God's Word until it becomes one with your spirit, soul, and mind. When that happens, you don't have to think about righteousness, you simply become what you already are inwardly by faith—the righteousness of God in Christ.

Too many saints have to slow down and think because they have made the mind their authority—the mind should simply function *automatically* like a drink machine. Your mind asks, "What did God say about that?" The Holy Spirit "pulls the answer up from memory" automatically and there it is revealed in your words and deeds.

We see it in Matthew 16 when Jesus asked the disciples:

> "'Who do men say that I, the Son of Man, am?' So they said, 'Some say John the Baptist, some Elijah, and others Jeremiah or one of the prophets.' He said to them, 'But who do you say that I am?' Simon Peter answered and said, 'You are the Christ, the Son of the living God.' Jesus answered and said to him, 'Blessed are you, Simon Bar-Jonah, for flesh and blood has not revealed this to you, but My Father who is in heaven'" (Mt. 16:13b-17).

Jesus was saying, "Blessed are you Simon Bar-Jonah because you didn't think this up."

We Are Too Much Like the Eleven—Head Over Heart

So what is our problem in the church? We are too much like the eleven *other* disciples. They valued their head over

136 their heart. They knew Jesus in the head but evidently they didn't know and recognize Him for who He was in the heart. That isn't something you can study.

You can't go to a Christian bookstore and just study it, or attend a seminar and absorb the data. You must spend some time with Him personally in the secret place.

When people ask me, "How am I really gonna know that God is real?" I tell them I don't have time to "convince" them about God's existence. He *assumes* we have enough sense to know He exists, or we wouldn't be asking. Whether it is the Gospel of John or the book of Genesis, the narrative begins, "In the beginning God...."

Faith in God is just that—it is a *faith* thing. I promise people who are seeking this kind of confirmation, "I will pray this for you—'God give this one an unmistakable experience, a divine encounter that will demonstrate beyond a doubt that You are God. Then all doubts will cease, and it will be *known* without mistake or hesitation that You alone are God.'"

Peter received a divine revelation of Jesus as God's Son because he had spent enough time with Him to know in his human spirit who Jesus really was.

It did not happen overnight. Once it happened, Jesus literally changed his name from Simon to Peter (the "Rock"). Even that new identity required intimacy and time to be revealed.

Peter was flaky and half-hearted all the way through the Lord's arrest, the suffering, and the cross. But the further revelation of Jesus and the arrival of the Holy Spirit on the Day of Pentecost *transformed* the flaky disciple into Peter the rock.

Meditating On Magazines, Talk shows and Trash TV

Your life will change once you rediscover what our grandmothers knew in the "old church," when you can declare your faith with the words, "I know that I know that I know!" It is time for us to stop trying to "do" the right thing and just "be" sons and daughters of God in *the image of Christ*. (Hint: It won't happen if we keep *meditating* on magazines, gossip tabloids, and trash television!)

God's Word said it best: "Let this mind be in you which was also in Christ Jesus" (Phil. 2:5). What was the "abundance of the heart" that came out of Jesus' mouth in times of crisis and temptation? *It is written... it is written....*

Do you want to start over? Follow in the footsteps and image of Jesus: "I must work the works of Him who sent Me while it is day; the night is coming when no one can work" (John 9:4).

Do what God says; don't stall and delay while you think about whether or not His commands are good things to do. God said:

> "'For My thoughts are not your thoughts, nor are your ways My ways,' says the Lord. 'For as the heavens are higher than the earth, so are My ways higher than your ways, and My thoughts than your thoughts'" (Isa. 55:8-9).

Don't even think about it. Just do it. No matter where you are or what difficulty you are facing right now, it is nothing compared to eternity.

What you do now determines how you will live in eternity. You have a divine mission, and the only way you can discern and understand your mission is to meditate on God's Word. Then He will make your way prosperous and give you good success.

Guard your thoughts and heart motivations. God has provided everything you need for a new beginning and fresh start in Christ. Now carefully guard your life and stay on track in God's Kingdom.

I constantly catch my mind thinking about things it

shouldn't be thinking about. It can easily rob me of my perfect peace in God. God has given us a foolproof guideline for guarding our hearts and minds:

> "Finally, brethren, whatever things are true, whatever things are noble, whatever things are just, whatever things are pure, whatever things are lovely, whatever things are of good report, if there is any virtue and if there is anything praiseworthy; *meditate on these things"* (Phil. 4:8, emphasis mine).

Too many of us suffer from "daily news head syndrome" and "night-time TV brain drain" symptoms. Are you sick of where you are? Are you tired of meditating on "Adam stuff"? Change your diet. Meditate only on Jesus Christ, the life-giving Spirit.

Your first assignment is to seek Him first. If you do that, you will have plenty of life, and divine anointing for your family, your church, and the strangers God sends your way. Remember, if you need to start over and you are feeling overwhelmed, pull up God's Word and allow the truth to set you free:

> "Repent therefore and be converted, that your sins may be blotted out, so that *times of refreshing may come from the presence of the Lord,* and that He may send Jesus Christ, who was preached to you before" (Acts 3:19-20, emphasis mine).

Endnotes

1. I have no interest in promoting one computer program over another, but I do want to communicate a truth to you in the best way possible. The literal word processing file I am

referring to ("WORD") is MicrosoftWord, a copyrighted and **139**
continuously upgraded software product developed and mar-
keted by Microsoft Corporation.

2. The specific NKJV references for meditate and meditating are Gen. 24:63, Josh. 1:8, Ps. 4:4; 5:1; 9:16; 19:14; 49:3;
63:6; 64:1; 77:6, 12; 104:34; 119:15, 27, 48, 78, 97, 99, 148;
143:5; 145:5; Isa. 33:18; Mal. 3:16; Luke 21:14; Phil. 4:8; 1
Tim. 4:15.

3. *Strong, Strong's Exhaustive Concordance of the Bible,*
Hebrew, #1897. hagah, haw-gaw'; a prim. root [comp.
H1901]; to murmur (in pleasure or anger); by impl. to ponder:--imagine, meditate, mourn, mutter, roar, X sore, speak,
study, talk, utter.

4. Ibid, Hebrew, #8104. shamar, shaw-mar'; a prim. root;
prop. to hedge about (as with thorns), i.e. guard; gen. to protect, attend to, etc.:--beware, be circumspect, take heed (to
self), keep (-er, self), mark, look narrowly, observe, preserve,
regard, reserve, save (self), sure, (that lay) wait (for), watch (-
man).

5. Ibid, Hebrew, #6743. tsalach, tsaw-lakh'; or tsa-leach,
tsaw-lay'-akh; a prim. root; to push forward, in various senses
(lit. or fig., trans. or intrans.):--break out, come (mightily), go
over, be good, be meet, be profitable, (cause to, effect, make
to, send) prosper (-ity, -ous, -ously).

6. Ibid, Hebrew, #7919. sakal, saw-kal'; a prim. root; to be
(caus. make or act) circumspect and hence intelligent:--con-
sider, expert, instruct, prosper, (deal) prudent (-ly), (give) skill
(-ful), have good success, teach, (have, make to) understand (-
ing), wisdom, (be, behave self, consider, make) wise (-ly),
guide wittingly.

Chapter 11
Change Begins With Change

Deliver me from Adam!

Deliverance from something begins when you deliver yourself to someone. Even a demonized man driven and harassed for years by up to 6,000 demons[1] discovered that he still had the power to seek out and fall at the feet of Jesus, the Prince of Peace (see Mark 5:9, Luke 8:30).

In other words, even the combined power of 6,000 demons is powerless to stop you from reaching out to Jesus. That means the key to *change in your life* is in your hands. No matter what circumstances you face right now, a turnaround and change of image is only one decision and one word away!

David was the great king, warrior, and psalmist of Israel. We still read, sing and pray the psalms he wrote under the inspiration of God. He was at the peak of his success and strength when he sinned with Bathsheba and fell from the heights of God's blessings to the level of becoming a murderer, adulterer, and betrayer.

If those events happened today, then David's story would dominate the evening news, the radio talk shows, and the prime time investigative news magazine programs for weeks! His sins were public knowledge, so there was no place to run and nowhere to hide.

How could a man come back from such a "grave" of failure and disgrace? He had committed adultery and then coolly plotted the death of Bathsheba's husband, Uriah the Hittite. This man was actually one of David's elite "thirty mighty men," known for his extreme loyalty, and chosen as a bodyguard to the king! (See 2 Sam. 23:39.)

142 He Confessed His Sin and Ignited the Power of Change

David changed and started over the same way you and I have to do it—through genuine repentance from the heart. He openly confessed his sin to God and ignited the power of change in his life with prayer and repentance:

> "Have mercy upon me, O God, according to Your lovingkindness; according to the multitude of Your tender mercies, blot out my transgressions. Wash me thoroughly from my iniquity, and cleanse me from my sin. *For I acknowledge my transgressions,* and my sin is always before me...
>
> "...*Purge me with hyssop,* and I shall be clean; *wash me,* and I shall be whiter than snow...
>
> "...*Create in me a clean heart, O God, and renew a steadfast spirit within me..."* (Ps. 51:1-3, 7, 10, emphasis mine).

Change begins when *you* begin to change, and godly change always begins on the inside.

My wife and I went through a Bible study together based on Rick Warren's book, *The Purpose Driven Life.*[2]

The Bible principles in that particular book were so solid and fundamental to godly living that I began to meditate on them. Before long, I reached the point where those scriptural principles began to alter my way of thinking.

Then I began to see different ways in which those truths were actually *changing me* from the inside, which in turn began to change things on the outside.

God gently reminded me personally through the Word that I am not a "mistake" or some accident that occurred by chance on the earth. It also became clearer to me than ever before that "It isn't about me, it is about God."

Committed to Transparent Ministry

I am committed to live and minister *transparently* before my congregation and my ministry leaders. When God reveals a character flaw or mistake that needs attention, I often make it a part of my message and I let my people track my progress in the process.

In my experience, transparent living on my part helps people see the way God works in a practical way. It also makes it easier for them to receive from me and yield to God's work in their own lives.

In other words, it is healthy for church members to see their leaders *changing* under the influence of God's Word and the Holy Spirit.

None of us have "arrived" at perfection in this life, but God expects *all of us* to pursue that goal in Christ's image. Even Paul told his followers and disciples, "Imitate me, just as I also imitate Christ" (1 Cor. 11:1).

For this reason, I challenged my congregation to change with me:

> *"I hope you all are all excited about change because I am hungry for God's abundant life. Jesus said He came so that I could have life, 'and that more abundantly' so I believe Him, and I am determined to live it. So I might as well take some folks with me. Everybody who wants to go, come on!*

> *"I have to tell you that as long as you are sitting under my leadership and walking with me as your pastor, you are going to change. You can't help but change! How can I be so sure? I'll tell you why—it is because I am changing. The best way for me to change someone else is for me to change."*

When You Grow, Those Around You Will Grow Too!

I tell the men in my church, "If you want your wife to be

better, then be a better husband. If you want your children to be better, then be a better father." Anytime you grow, then the people around you will tend to grow too. This excites me as a leader and as a Christian.

Jesus was serious when He said, "I've come that you might have life and have it more abundantly." I am determined to find out what that really is and then experience it! When I think about it, I haven't seen very many people who have actually walked in and lived out "the abundant life."

The abundant life really begins with change. And change begins when *you* begin to change. Every time I've prayed about difficult or painful challenges I'm facing, I noticed that God doesn't drop everything to "fix it" right then.

Now I know that He could, and I know that He would if it was best for me. However, I also learned that most of the time, He didn't change things and wouldn't change them until I began to change first.

It almost seems to me that God was saying through His methods:

> *"Eddie, I am going to change you first, so you can deal with the problem just in case I don't change it. When you have changed enough to deal with it, the problem won't bother you anymore...and that is when I will change it."*

The bottom-line version of this principle is this: If you want something changed in your life, you should get delivered from it first. Then you can pray with a pure heart, "Thank you, Lord. If you don't change it, then I am *still* going to be happy, I am still going to walk in joy, and I am still going to get the abundant life."

That is when God will probably say, "Okay, I can fix that now. You are going up to the next level, so I can give you what you need."

One of the biggest sources of unhappiness in life is our self- defeating habit of focusing on things we can't change. We should be celebrating what has been dealt to us today! We should also be thinking about how we can change the things we have the power to change.

Most of us Focus on our Problems

The first and most important thing you can change is your attitude. Secondly, you can change your focus—what are you thinking about most of the time? Most of us get sour or defeated attitudes because we focus on our problems (and as a result reap more of the same).

We obsessively ponder all of the things we don't have or the financial problems we do have. Then we get lost in our compulsive thought about the physical attributes we don't have (slender and muscular bodies, a full head of hair, an attractive face, a certain color of eyes, skin, or hair); or the physical problems we do have (such as cancer, obesity, multiple sclerosis, a physical deformity, or a birth defect).

Focus on the things you can change—beginning with you! You can't change your height, but you can develop a thankful heart for every inch God gave you and make the most of it!

God gave us a checklist for maximum health in our thought lives. We need to pull out this Five Point Checklist everyday for a thinking checkup from the neck up:

> Number 1: Be anxious for nothing, but in everything by prayer and supplication, with thanksgiving, let your requests be made known to God;
> Number 2: and the peace of God, which surpasses all understanding, will guard your hearts and minds through Christ Jesus.
> Number 3: Finally, brethren, whatever things are true, whatever things are noble, whatever things

are just, whatever things are pure, whatever things are lovely, whatever things are of good report, if there is any virtue and if there is anything praiseworthy; meditate on these things.

Number 4: The things which you learned and received and heard and saw in me, these do,

Number 5: and the God of peace will be with you (Phil. 4:6-9, emphasis mine).

That is the way to use the power of the mind for effective change. God the creator never designed us to think about and meditate upon bad things we cannot change. He does cause us to remember past mistakes and trials so we can avoid them in the future—but those are things we have the power to change.

Change Yourself So Your Circumstances Will Change

The day Moses died, God assigned the leadership of Israel to Joshua and gave him a prescription to help an entire nation change *themselves* so their circumstances would change as well.

We've looked at this passage before, but it deserves another look because these words were addressed to a man who had wandered in the wilderness for 40 years. Joshua was now one of the two oldest people in the group, and he could still remember the bondage of Egypt.

Joshua had a big job ahead of him, and this is how God prepared him for the task. First God told him to cross the River Jordan with all of the people. Then He made three personal promises to Joshua (very similar to individual promises we have in His Word today).

God told Joshua that every place he walked would be given to him, and secondly, that no one would be able to withstand him in his lifetime (see Josh. 1:2, 5). Finally He made a promise that is exactly identical to the promise Jesus made to

us in the New Testament: "I will be with you. I will not leave
you nor forsake you" (see Josh. 1:5b, Heb. 13:5 and
Mt. 28:20b).

God's Practical and Tactical Commands For Success

Then God gave Joshua some practical or tactical commands for success that had to do with his *thinking patterns:*

> *"Be strong and of good courage,* for to this people
> you shall divide as an inheritance the land which I swore
> to their fathers to give them. *Only be strong and very
> courageous,* that you may *observe* to do according to all
> the law which Moses My servant commanded you; *do
> not turn from it to the right hand or to the left,* that you
> may prosper wherever you go. *This book of the Law shall
> not depart from your mouth,* but you shall *meditate in it
> day and night,* that you may *observe to do* according to
> all that is written in it. *For then you will make your way
> prosperous, and then you will have good success.* Have I
> not commanded you? Be strong and of good courage; do
> not be afraid, nor be dismayed, for the LORD your God
> is with you wherever you go" (Josh. 1:6-9, emphasis
> mine).

If you think about things long enough, and if you *do* something often enough, those things become a part of you. Jesus
was consumed with love for His Father and zeal for His
Father's house. He and the Father were one, and He prayed
that we would come to the same level of unity, union, and
joint identity (see John 17).

Jesus Focused on His Father's Desire

Even though Jesus knew that obedience would lead to
brutal beatings, public humiliation, and painful death on
a cross, He focused on His Father's desire and prayed:

"Father, if it is Your will, take this cup away from Me; nevertheless *not My will, but Yours, be done*" (Luke 22:42, emphasis mine).

Jesus was saying, "Father, if it's for me to deal with this bitter cup, then I will do it. This isn't about Me, it is all about You and blessing others. If I save Myself but fail to bless others, then My living is in vain."

At the very end of His ordeal on the cross, Jesus did something that should set the standard for all of us who have been hurt or "done wrong" by somebody else. He refused to strike out or strike back in the image of Adam. He answered for all of us in the image of God, "Father, forgive them, for they do not know what they do" (see Luke 23:34).

We rarely do what Jesus did because we are too busy propping up and protecting our egos, and clinging to our grudges, offenses, and vows of vengeance. Some us are so ensnared in Adam's fallen image, we are still angry at people for things that happened 10, 20, or sometimes 60 years ago!

There are saints in their 80's who are *still* angry and bitter over wrongs they suffered before they were 10 years old! How can this be? How can any of us refuse to forgive others after all that God did to forgive us?

Want Trouble? Allow Your Mind to Run Things

All you have to do is allow your mind to run things, which means it keeps reminding you and reinforcing the emotions you felt each and every time you were wronged or offended.

It happens to sinner and saint alike and there is only one cure—you must exchange the death-giving image of Adam for the life-giving Spirit found only in Christ, the last Adam.

Change begins when you begin to change.

So how do you relate to Jesus and what He has done? Once you choose to change, you begin by identifying personally with what Jesus did on the cross. According to God's Word, **149** the power of change is directly linked to what the Lord accomplished for us on Calvary:

> "For the death that He died, He died to sin once for all; but the life that He lives, He lives to God. Likewise you also, *reckon yourselves to be dead indeed to sin,* but *alive to God* in Christ Jesus our Lord" (Rom. 6:10-11, emphasis mine).

When Paul told the Roman Christians to "reckon your-selves to be dead indeed to sin'" he was saying, "Consider yourself dead—sin can't even touch you. Count yourself as a dead man, unmoved and uninterested in the best that sin has to offer."

If you ask some people in the church, this Bible verse may as well be written in the original Greek language. They just can't "get" it.

It's Time to Renovate, Clean, Rebuild, and Make New

They had better try again, because this truth is at the core of God's "change-your-life program." The Bible commands us, "be *renewed* in the spirit of your mind" (Eph. 4:23, empha-sis mine).

The original Greek word translated as renewed means "to renovate."[3] Someone special has set up residence in your heart and is sharing space in your mind. It is time *to renovate, to clean, rebuild, and make new.*

Jesus shows us how His Word is involved in the renovation process in the way He deals with the church:

> "Husbands, love your wives, *just as Christ also loved the church* and *gave* Himself for her, that He might *sanctify and cleanse her with the washing of water by the word"* (Eph. 5:25-26).

So we renew, make new, or renovate our minds by "washing" it with the life-giving, sin-cleansing water of God's Word. Can you see how this truth just might help "reprogram" your mind for daily living? This means God is at work in you, changing your image supernaturally. Your part is to "take a bath" regularly in God's Word.

This work of God in our lives was a central theme in the Apostle Paul's life and ministry. It seems something on the subject of godly change or taking on the image of Christ showed up in almost every letter he wrote.

Paul told his younger disciple, Timothy, about a faithful saying that describes the outcome or result of our decisions and actions in Christ:

> **"This is a faithful saying: For if we died with Him, we shall also live with Him. If we endure, we shall also reign with Him. If we deny Him, He also will deny us. If we are faithless, He remains faithful; He cannot deny Himself"** (2 Tim. 2:11-13).

In simplified form, we see how faith in the Lord's faithfulness directly affects our life and destiny:
- If we died with Him—we shall also live with Him.
- If we endure [in this earthly life]—we shall also reign with Him [now in this life *and* in the life to come].
- If we deny Him [here on earth], He also will deny us [before the Father in heaven].
- If we are faithless, He *remains* faithful; He cannot deny Himself.

As always, the Lord is interested in our actions and motives of the heart, not just in our words. When Jesus talked with people about repentance, He said: "Bring forth therefore fruits *meet* for repentance" (Mt. 3:8, KJV, emphasis mine). That means your daily life should match up with the change you claim has taken place in your heart.

God set the high bar for evidence of change in John's letter to the churches. If you have really begun to change; if genuine change is coming to your life, then there should be some light in your life—especially in the areas where you have struggled with darkness.

> **"If we say that we have fellowship with Him, and walk in darkness, we lie and do not practice the truth. But *if we walk in the light as He is in the light* [if we walk in His image instead of Adam's dark image], we have fellowship with one another, and the blood of Jesus Christ His Son *cleanses us from all sin*" (1 John 1:6-7, emphasis mine).**

If we mean it when we cry out to God, "Deliver me from Adam," then we won't wait around for some miraculous event like the parting of the sea or the arrival of an angel in a bright beam of light.

Godly change begins the moment you *choose* to say yes to God. You ignite outward change instantly when you change your heart and mind and begin to *do* what God says in His Word. Your situation may not turn around instantly, but the process of change begins the moment you choose Christ's image over Adam.

Above all, don't be discouraged. The Bible says, "...it is God who works in you both to will and to do for His good pleasure" (Phil. 2:13, emphasis mine). He put the desire in your heart for change, and He will help you "do" what it takes to change.

Sometimes I do things in our church services to drive home key points. One time I told the people, "Grab somebody and say, '*Baby, if you could see your future!*'"

Change can be stressful, but it is much easier if we can get a vision for what is to come. Even Jesus found it easier to endure the pain of the cross because He had a vision.

The writer of Hebrews told us to look "...unto Jesus, the author and finisher of our faith, *who for the joy that was set before Him* endured the cross, despising the shame, and has sat

152 down at the right hand of the throne of God" (Heb. 12:2).

Begin the change now. Focus on what God's Word tells you to do, and believe only what *He* says about you rather than what your past or your circumstances say. See it through—all the way through.

> "Behold, I stand at the door and knock. If anyone hears My voice and opens the door, I will come in to him and dine with him, and he with Me. To him who overcomes I will grant to sit with Me on My throne, as I also overcame and sat down with My Father on His throne" (Rev. 3:20-21).

Endnotes

1. Merrill F. Unger, *Unger's Bible Dictionary* (Chicago, Moody Press, 1966), p. 653. "Legion, a main division of the Roman army, nearly equivalent to our regiment. It comprised a much larger number of men, running from three thousand to about six thousand at the time of Christ...legion came to mean a great number or multitude."

2. Rick Warren, *The Purpose Driven Life: What Am I Here For?* (Grand Rapids, MI: Zondervan, 2002).

3. *Strong, Strong's Exhaustive Concordance of the Bible,* Greek, #365. ananeoo, an-an-neh-o'-o; from G303 and a der of H3501; to renovate; i.e. reform:–renew.

Chapter 12

A New Dimension: The Image of God

You were created in the image of God, but you inherited Adam's image in your soul. Which image wins in your life?

Settle the question in your heart of who you are—and *whose* you are. Once that point is settled, you will begin to "go on automatic."

When the image of the old Adam is crucified and buried at the cross; when you emerge from the new birth as a new creature formed in the image of Christ, then this new image dwelling within you rises up *automatically.*

Why? Because it is who you are. The old you in the image of the first Adam is dead. You have risen in the last Adam, so now "you just *be.*"

People will notice you just as they noticed Peter and John. Those supposedly ignorant fishermen were hauled in front of the Jewish Sanhedrin or ruling council and ordered to stop preaching Christ.

They "went automatic" and suddenly began to preach and defend the faith with divine authority and boldness—even though these were the same leaders and the same council that had just condemned Jesus Christ and turned Him over to the Romans for crucifixion!

The Bible says the spiritual rulers of Israel "marveled" about the transformation they saw in Peter and John:

> "Now when they saw the boldness of Peter and John, and perceived that they were uneducated and untrained men, they marveled. *And they realized that they had been with Jesus.* And seeing the man who had

been healed standing with them, they could say nothing against it. But when they had commanded them to go aside out of the council, they conferred among themselves, saying, *'What shall we do to these men?'"* (Acts 4:13-16).

When something is inside you—when it is a *part* of you—it can't help but show up automatically.

A Linebacker Among Mostly Godly Gladiators

I was a very successful linebacker when I played football earlier in my life. When our church fellowship planned a football game, we had three weeks to practice and prepare for the match-up of the "mostly godly gladiators."

I was only able to attend one of those practices, but it did not disturb my team. Why? Because they know that I am athletic, and they know my reputation. When I entered the game, everything about being a linebacker came back to me automatically.

When the ball was snapped, I knew how to read the quarterback. I knew when to go left, when to go right, when to lay back and pursue, and when to rush the quarterback.

I didn't "think" about what a linebacker does because it was just me—*I just be* (pardon my English slang, but I have a hunch the construction of these words closely matches Greek sentence construction).

You Just Do It!

In the natural realm, you don't think about anything you are good at doing—you just do it! In the realm of the spirit, you don't "think" about being God's adopted son or daughter —*you just be.* If you have to think about it, then you may just talk yourself out of it because you don't know Him well enough.

Michael Jordan didn't have to "think" about how to slam-dunk a basketball. I'm positive that Tiger Woods does not stand on the gold green "thinking" to himself, *Now how do I swing a golf club again?* Tiger is golf! He wrote a whole new standard for golf at an early age.

Why? Because he has golfed so much since childhood that he can wake up in the middle of the night, rub his eyes, put a golf ball on a tee and knock it 400 and some odd feet—and still get it to go pretty much where he wants it to go!

He doesn't "think" about it. He could drop another ball and...*bam!* Drop another ball and...bam! He doesn't have to stand there hoping he can just keep the ball on the green (like some of us do who play golf once every 6 months).

A young Christian is just learning about the image of Christ, so they don't know how to position themselves. With time, knowledge in the Word of God, and a growing relationship with Jesus, it can all become automatic.

The walk from spiritual infancy to spiritual maturity involves more than "buying your ticket to Heaven." God our Father made it clear that He is after sons and daughters, not mere robots or religious followers. In fact, your personal destiny is eternally linked to the *image* of Jesus Christ.

The Bible says, "For whom [God] foreknew, He also predestined to be *conformed to the image of His Son,* that He might be the firstborn among many brethren" (Rom. 8:29, emphasis mine).

It Is Time to Move On and Move Up

This is why I am so determined to encourage you to move on and move up from the image of the first Adam to the image of the last Adam. You are called, anointed, and destined to identify with and operate as Christ in the earth. That is why He called you to take up your cross and follow Him, not merely watch Him or read about Him (see Luke 9:23). Think of it this way:

- In Adam, all things die. In Christ, all things are made alive.
- I am in Christ. Therefore, I live.
- Adam became a living being, but Christ became a life-giving spirit.
- I am in Christ. Therefore, I am a life-giving spirit.

Jesus Christ operates in a totally different dimension than Adam did. We must understand this if we ever hope to understand the battle that takes place between the "old man of the flesh" or the first Adam, and the new creature formed in the image of Christ.

Paul the apostle put it this way:

"For *if you live according to the flesh you will die;* but if by the Spirit you put to death the deeds of the body, *you will live.* For as many as are led by the Spirit of God, *these are sons of God.* For you did not receive the spirit of bondage again to fear, but you received the Spirit of adoption by whom we cry out, 'Abba, Father.' The Spirit Himself bears witness with our spirit that *we are children of God, and if children, then heirs; heirs of God and joint heirs with Christ,* if indeed we suffer with Him, that we may also be glorified together" (Rom. 8:13-17, emphasis mine).

Simply Operating in the Image of God

We are to walk by faith and not by sight or merely according to our five human senses. There are some who prosper and succeed because of *what they see in the Spirit.* Their success did not come from what they saw or did in the physical and natural realm. They dared to call those things out of the *invisible* into the *visible.*

This is simply *operating in the image of God*—nothing more and nothing less.

The Bible makes it clear that you and I existed long before **157** we could be seen by the unaided human eye. God told one man, "Before I formed you in the womb I knew you; before you were born I sanctified you" (Jer. 1:5, emphasis mine). God is no respecter of persons (see Acts 10:34), so we know this same truth applies to every human being born of a woman.

The book of Genesis also tells us that we were originally created in God's image and likeness, and that He gave the first Adam dominion over the earth. We were able—and in fact, God *commanded us*—to rule, subdue, and have dominion over the earth and everything in it (see Gen. 1:26-28).

God hasn't changed His mind. Jesus Christ "reconnected" us with God. The things God did for us were in the Spirit, and you have to *see it* to bring it into the natural realm.

Our Actions Reflect Our Choices

The reason we are so broken down and torn down, and the reason we talk down and "think down" so much is because we live primarily by our natural senses—we "walk in the flesh." The choice is ours. *We* choose what we think about and *meditate* upon, and our actions faithfully reflect our choices.

"For those who *live according to the flesh* set their minds on the things of the flesh, but those who *live according to the Spirit,* the things of the Spirit. For to be carnally minded is death, but to be spiritually minded is life and peace" (Rom 8:5-6, emphasis mine).

God is saying, "Walk in the Spirit" (see Ezek. 36:27, Gal. 5:16, 25). Most of the things that we call our "problems" aren't really our problems. They are our focus, and they gain more power in our lives the more attention we devote to them. It is time to enter a new dimension through the image of Christ.

158   Too many people in the church live in fear, and their focus on the flesh keeps them from using the training God has given them *to move boldly into new areas and to fulfill their God-given dreams.*

Great business people study biblical business principles until those truths become so intertwined with their spirits that they can't help themselves! In due season, they absorb a deep understanding of the principle, "To receive is to give."

It Pours From Their Spirits Automatically

They can't help but plunge their lives into a ministry of giving! Their understanding and grasp of godly business principles aren't based in their heads—it pours out from their spirits *automatically.*

This triggers the blessing originally given to Abraham and passed on to all who walk in the image of Christ by faith:[1]

". . . if you diligently...observe carefully all His commandments...all these blessings shall come upon you and overtake you...Blessed shall you be in the city, and blessed shall you be in the country. Blessed shall be the fruit of your body, the produce of your ground and the increase of your herds... Blessed shall be your basket and your kneading bowl. Blessed shall you be when you come in, and blessed shall you be when you go out. The Lord will cause your enemies who rise against you to be defeated before your face; they shall come out against you one way and flee before you seven ways. The Lord will command the blessing on you in your storehouses and in all to which you set your hand..."

"The Lord will open to you His good treasure, the heavens, to give the rain to your land in its season, and to bless all the work of your hand. You shall lend to many nations, but you shall not borrow. And the Lord

will make you the head and not the tail; you shall be   **159**
above only, and not be beneath..." (Deut. 28:1-8, 12-
13, emphasis mine).

This covenant promise was an *image-changing* promise
from God to a man of faith. Very few human beings have ever
really entered into this promise. This covenant was delivered
to Abraham thousands of years ago, and later covenant
blessings given to Moses and David revealed a new dimension
of life in God's favor.

Our new covenant in Christ is an even better covenant,
including but far exceeding any of these divine covenants
made between God and man (see Heb. 8:6). In Christ, we
literally take on the image of the living God!

Every year we live on this earth, our need for deliverance
from Adam grows more urgent. Why? Because each new day
can bring new hurts and fresh memory clips that can entangle
and imprison us if we continue to struggle on in the image of
Adam.

Making Myself Vulnerable Before the Lord

Even as I write these words, I am making myself
vulnerable before the Lord, because all I want is for God to fix
me and make me pleasing in His sight. It is this kind of "assist-
ed humbling" that allows me to die to "self" daily, so I can
correct myself and align my thinking with God's Word.

Life lived in the image of Christ is a life of freedom and
abundance! In Christ, I live and move and have my being!
I am determined to live in Him, and when the time comes for
my family, friends, and parishioners to celebrate my home-
going, I want them to say, "That fellow, now he *lived!*"

I've told my wife and family to make sure that *while*
my funeral is going on at New Birth Missionary Baptist
Church, that what is left of me is allowed to take a final ride

160 around the City of Atlanta on Interstate 285 with an escort of six police motorcycles and a helicopter. (I'll snarl traffic and deliver my last "wave" to Atlanta while my church family celebrates my home-going).

In Christ, I am determined to live with no regrets and go out in style. Even my home-going should say to the world, "This is the way a child of God, king, and priest leaves this world—in the image, the blessing, and the joy of the Lord!"

It Isn't Something We "Do"—it is Someone We "Are"

Does this sound strange to you? Today may be my last day, or it may be your final day of life. In any case, we should live and leave this life in Christ's image, with no regrets. It isn't something we "do," it is who we "are."

If you are having trouble grasping this truth, the problem may be some of the traditions you inherited in life. I am determined to tear down all fleshly church tradition that is needless and that hinders us from walking in what God has ordained.

I am a son of a Baptist preacher, so I have been in church all my life. (I haven't been saved all of my life, but I have been in church all of my life.)

I've heard some of the greatest preaching you could ever hear, and I've had some great experiences in church meetings, but I detected a disturbing pattern over the course of time. I noticed that there are certain things that we do in church that are not moving us into the next dimension with God.

Most of those things "feel good" because we have been doing them all along as habits rather than things revealed in God's Word. Many of us will admit that our greatest frustration has been rooted in the lack of power we see in all of this. "Okay, so I come to church and I worship. Why aren't things changing as they should?"

Once again, it is because we are "doing" church instead

of "being" what God ordained for us to be. You cannot "do" **161** it—you have to "be" it.

We know that God isn't wrong, so if something is not working right, that means that you and I as followers of Christ need to make some adjustments. Most people have a deep dislike for change, but when change is needed, it is far better to at least try something to be in the will of God than to bury your head in the sand of apathy.

Release the Holy Ghost to Take Hold of You

Half of the job is done once you decide you are going to walk the way God wants you to walk. That releases the Holy Ghost to take hold of you and say, "I've been waiting for your permission to move in the things the Father has ordained for your life!"

Do you recognize the dimension you are in right now?

Seasons are temporary. I don't want you to fall into the mindset that says, "I am about to move into a temporary blessing." No, you are about to move into a permanent dimension unlike any you have experienced. When you understand this, you will walk in what God ordained and not settle for second-best. I am convinced that we are all very close to something in God.

Don't get discouraged to the point where you want to throw in the towel. Ask yourself why this pressure is pressing on you—is it because you have become so focused on the Kingdom of God that the devil is getting upset? His problem—and your blessing—is that you have already come too far to turn around. You cannot lose!

Earlier we mentioned the book of Job, and the way Job persevered by faith through incredible loss. In the end, God restored to him *double* for everything he lost. It was Job who said it so plainly: "Naked I came from my mother's womb, and naked shall I return there. The Lord gave, and the Lord has taken away; blessed be the name of the Lord" (Job 1:21).

Is God Making Room for Something New?

You may be facing a major loss, or your circumstances may look so bad that you may lose everything you have. Be encouraged and remember Job: When God starts moving a whole lot of stuff out of your life, check out the end of the Book of Job. God may be making room for something new in a new *dimension!*

There was a time when my wife and I moved to a different house from the one we had been living in. The first house was a pretty good place to live, but we had a good opportunity to purchase something nicer, and we took it.

I picked up the phone to rent a moving truck to move our stuff when my wife interrupted me.

"Wait," she said. "What are you doing?"

"I'm renting a moving truck, because we need to move this stuff." I said.

"Oh no," she said.

"Why?"

"That stuff was for that house," she said, "but it isn't going to fit in this house."

She must have seen the "This Does Not Compute" light go on because she took a minute to carefully explain the concept to me.

"Eddie, this house has to have new stuff because it is a *different* house. We can't take old stuff in there because that old sofa has some old memories I don't want to take with us. This chair has some memories I don't want to deal with. *There is some stuff here that just won't fit where we're going.* It doesn't say what we're about to say in our new place, so we have to start fresh."

It Won't Fit Because It Doesn't Belong

Listen: I have to tell you that the "stuff" you use to lay in—the stuff that use to make you comfortable instead of making you Christ-like—isn't going into the new dimension God has for you. It won't fit because it doesn't belong.

You already know you have moved. The problem is that **163** you keep trying to carry in all the old furniture when God is saying:

"No, you can't take that. Look, I am going to unload your truck of furniture, and I will not let you move the truck until you get everything out of it.

"Now I want you to understand that you don't need the truck anyway. Where I'm taking you, the old won't do. Don't try to put this new dimension [the new wine] in the old [old wineskins]. I am buying you a whole new house full of furniture that will exactly fit your new home. You don't know it, but where you are going, you will need two dishwashers to keep up. [You have to see this in the Spirit.]

"Where you are going, you need another apartment in your house. You will need some things that you haven't even thought about or heard of—but I did" [see 1 Cor. 2:9].

Trust Him and Go With the Flow

Did your family ever move to a new house or a new town when you were a child? If they did, then you know what it feels like to be uncertain about what your parents were doing—all you could do was trust them and go with the flow.

God our Father is doing some things that we don't understand. If He does reveal some of His plans, it is certain that you won't understand it all.

He may tell you to "get away from your kinfolk" as He did to Abraham, or separate you from your lifelong friends for a season. He may send you into a wilderness to wear skins and live on bugs, or He may place you in a working relationship with someone who just can't stand you.

Peter loved Jesus, but he also tried *sincerely* to love Jesus out of His divine purpose. He had zeal and love for Jesus, but very little understanding of the big picture. Jesus came to lay down His life on the cross, and Peter tried to stop the high priest's posse of soldiers. He even cut off the ear of the High Priest's servant with his sword! Jesus had to intervene, telling him to put away the sword.

In a twisted sense, Judas was doing the work of a real friend by facilitating the betrayal. Have you ever wondered why you can't pray away all of your devils? If you didn't have any pressure, you wouldn't pray! (And God wants you to pray now as never before!)

We Are in a New Dimension

When I preach on the blessings of God, I don't impart things just to help you get rich. We are in a new dimension. Responsibility comes with every blessing of God. *The purpose of this new dimension is to empower you.* It is for God to receive the glory and *not you.*

Why does God bring us out of so many ridiculous situations? It is so that He can get glory. That is why so many people know about your business and private affairs. God may allow other people to *know* your business so they will know there was no way you could get up or out on your own!

Just when they were sure you were going to snap, they wake up and see you walking in a *new dimension.* Perhaps they will experience the amazement the ruling council felt about Peter and John 2,000 years ago. *"And they realized that they had been with Jesus"* (Acts 4:15).

"Wait a minute. Is he the one who denied Jesus? Isn't this the one with the stutter, the one who never went to Bible college? Isn't she the one who couldn't read? Who taught her to read out of the Bible like that?"

Now, you have made it this far in this book. If you want to be delivered from Adam as I did, then you will have to go after it. Don't just sit back and assume your deliverance will just happen followed by a glorious encounter with the Lord.

Other People May Be Convinced You Are Crazy

You must be willing to be a *forerunner.* Unfortunately, that may mean you will walk in revelation and experiences that only you will see. Other people—including some members of your own family—may be convinced you are crazy. (If it happened to Jesus Christ, why wouldn't it happen to us?)

God will require you to take criticism from people with grace, knowing that if you succeed, they will all be blessed. Even when people around you act in massive stupidity and ignorance, you will be able to go *in the image of Christ,* knowing that God sent you and entrusted you with the responsibility of blessing others.

I encourage you to walk as God ordained you to walk, even though it is sometimes uncomfortable. Now pray this out loud with me:

"Lord, deliver me from Adam. I want to walk, live, and serve as you did. Anoint me to do it in Your image and in Your likeness, with dominion and authority." Amen.

When God blew His divine breath into the lifeless body of Adam, he became a living being. However, when you were filled with the Holy Ghost, you became a life-giving spirit.

May They Leave Your Presence Hungry For God

I declare right now that everyone who comes in contact with you will be so affected by the life-giving spirit within you that he or she will be drawn closer to Jesus Christ, lifted higher in his or her vision of God, and pulled deeper into the Kingdom of God.

Because God Almighty dwells within you, and the very image of Christ has transformed you, I declare that they can't help but witness the presence of the living God when they see and talk with you. May they leave your presence hungry for God, thirsty for His presence, and richer in spirit than when they first encountered you.

Remember that the Spirit of the Lord doesn't merely shine upon you. The incomparable Spirit of the Lord is shining *through* you. It is written, "Arise, shine; For your light has come! And the glory of the LORD is risen upon you" (Isa. 60:1).

Leave behind the fallen image of the first Adam and take up the image of the risen Christ. Allow the power of God to transform you in position, power, and purpose. I pronounce that at this moment, you are becoming the head and not the tail of every situation in this life.

We were created in the image of God, and now He has brought us to a new beginning point. Let the adventure begin.

"[You] have *put on the new man* who is renewed in knowledge *according to the image of Him* who created him" (Col. 3:10, emphasis mine).

Endnotes

1. Some may question whether or not God's promises to Abraham can be applied or enjoyed by other people—especially to non-Jewish people. The Bible tells us Jesus redeemed us from the curse of the Law: "that the blessing of Abraham might come upon the Gentiles in Christ Jesus, that we might receive the promise of the Spirit through faith" (Gal. 33:14).